The Unexpected Tour Guide

By
Jeff C. West

What Sales Leaders and Best Selling Authors Are Saying About

The Unexpected Tour Guide

"*The Unexpected Tour Guide* is full of wisdom and insights that will make you a better salesperson and a better person overall in every area of your life."

~ Brian Tracy, Bestselling Author of *Unlimited Sales Success*

"Brief, powerful and impactful. *The Unexpected Tour Guide* combines an entertaining story with some of the best teaching you'll ever receive on how to become a hugely successful sales professional. If you're in the selling profession, buy this book. If you're a sales manager or leader, buy one for your entire team and watch your sales numbers rise and rise."

~Bob Burg, Bestselling author of *Endless Referrals and Adversaries into Allies*

"Your life, your income, the results you're getting are nothing more than a mirror reflection of what you are putting forth. If you're unsatisfied with your current results, read *The Unexpected Tour Guide*. It will help you gain a new, improved perspective and find a more fulfilling direction."

~Tom Hopkins, Bestselling author of *How to Master the Art of Selling and When Buyers Say No* (with Ben Katt).

"*The Unexpected Tour Guide*" may very well be one of those stories you remember for the rest of your life. And if you apply the lessons it contains, it may lead you to one of the best stories yet to be written – yours."

~Paul S. Amos, II, President — Aflac

"*The Unexpected Tour Guide*; I couldn't put it down until I finished it. What a great little book. This short read tells a timeless story that will not only be impactful to those in sales or business, but to everyone in every walk of life. Jesus Christ taught through parables for a reason. Jeff West does the same with this gem of a story that will be life changing for all who read it. Thanks Jeff!"

~Michael J.Tomlinson, Senior Vice President, Director of Sales, Aflac

"I have read many books in my 35+ year sales career and this is one of the best. Jeff has written a book that can change your career but more importantly your life. He shares principles that are timely for the struggling salesperson but also the seasoned professional. Most important he helps us discover why we do what we do."

~Lynn G. Barnson,Market Director, Aflac-Utah

""*Just finished The Unexpected Tour Guide.* Thanks in advance from every salesman whose career will be successful because of it! Great story – laughed, cried, remembered"

-Eric Leger, Vice President - Aflac,
Southwest Territory

"At around 10:30 I began reading your book... I honestly couldn't put it down. The funny thing is that I never once considered putting it down and giving in to the temptation to sleep. Your messages are spot on and I truly enjoyed every chapter as the story unfolded. It's now 1:02 and I just had to send you a note of thanks."

~ Blaze Fremin, Market Director – Aflac, Louisiana

"Regardless of how motivated you may be, if you will read Jeff's book and do the exercises, you will become even more motivated and discover areas to develop to take you and your business to a higher level. *The Unexpected Tour Guide* will become a classic in the field of personal development."

~Mike Butler, Market Director – Aflac,
North Carolina

ISBN 978-0-9916223-1-3 (paperback)

ISBN 978-0-9916223-0-6 (cloth)

ISBN 978-0-9916223-2-0 (ebook)

LCCN: 2014933343

Printed in the USA by

The Sales Tour Guide Publishing

http://www.thesalestourguide.com

The Unexpected Tour Guide

A Salesman, A Homeless Man
And an Incredible Adventure

Foreword

by
Paul S. Amos, II, President Aflac
(American Family Life Assurance Company of Columbus, GA)

If you build your people, they will build their business.

I have witnessed firsthand the truth of that statement. My grandfather and his two brothers began a small insurance company in Columbus, GA in 1955. With high dreams and hard work they grew that business into what has become an international company on the Fortune 500® list with current assets exceeding $118 billion dollars. Not only did they build a business, they built an industry – the voluntary employee benefits industry.

The three Amos brothers did not accomplish this feat alone. They successfully attracted people to their organization – good people. They worked with those people. They taught them how to build their businesses. Then they encouraged them to use Aflac as the vehicle to accomplish the dreams and goals they had for their families. Countless people have done exactly that over the last 58 years.

Jeff West is one of those people.

I have known Jeff for most of his Aflac career. When Jeff started with Aflac in 1993, he and his family were in the midst of major financial difficulties. As a matter of fact, I have heard Jeff jokingly say, "If anyone had robbed me in the days before I began my career with Aflac – all they would have gotten was practice!" I have watched him as his business and his income grew exponentially over the last 21 years. He did so by developing his craft in sales and transferring that knowledge and skill set to others. Then he encouraged them to chase their dreams.

He built his people and they built their businesses.

Stories sell – and _The Unexpected Tour Guide_ is a great story. It is a story that will keep you engaged and will teach you great principles for life as well as sales. Read the story. Apply the lessons. Then reap a great return for the time and money you have invested.

The Unexpected Tour Guide may very well be one of those stories that you remember for the rest of your life. And if you apply the lessons it contains, it may lead you to one of the best stories yet to be written – yours.

Dedication

I have been blessed.

I have a beautiful wife who is patient with me, and is absolute proof that I am excellent in sales. I have two daughters who inspire me to be better, and with whom I have been hopelessly and helplessly in love since I first held them in my arms on the day of their births. And I have had a colorful cast of family and friends who have set excellent examples for me. Even though this work is fictional, bits and pieces from many of them are reflected in the development of the characters.

I have also been blessed with several wonderful mentors. There are too many to name them all, but I wanted to mention just a few such as Bill Ross in Peachtree City, Georgia, who taught me how to have fun as I built a business; and Billy Florence in Athens, Georgia, who taught me to build a business as I had fun. Although their influence was during my early adulthood, it no doubt has made me a better man today.

To my favorite authors: Dr. John Maxwell, who taught me how to be a leader; and Bob Burg, who taught me how to be a true giver, not only in his written words but by his actions with me and those around me.

But I want to dedicate this book to two particular mentors who will always hold very special places in my heart:

To the real Jack Amberson: You set the finest example of what a Godly man does in his work and family life. You gave me my first personal development book. You taught me how to work hard. And you taught me how a father loves his children. A young man, fresh out of college, could not have asked for better mentorship than I got from you. My life and the lives of my children are much richer because you have been a part of my story.

And to Frank Davies: You set the finest example of how a man can be passionate about his business. You taught me that you can't hide hard work. You taught me how to lead an organization with emotion, integrity, and enthusiasm. It is one of my greatest desires that I have passed along the things I learned from you to those in my charge.

Table of Contents

PROLOGUE

In the office of Jim Fariss – current day

Y ou and I have never met.

As we speak, I am sitting in my office, preparing for a meeting with a young man whom I believe has the potential to be one of the most impactful leaders in my company. He is intelligent, and has great people skills and a youthful enthusiasm that, if channeled in the right direction, could turn him into a star.

And yet he thinks he is coming to this meeting to be fired… for underperformance.

Who can blame him? His sales results thus far would certainly make that a foregone conclusion.

However, I have other plans for him.

But before I get into all of that, I think I should introduce myself.

*   *   *   *   *

My name is Jim Fariss, and I am the owner of a business that provides solutions to families in need of assistance when medical events create financial difficulties.

But, more importantly, I am the owner of an incredible story. It's the story of my life.

I'm not at all sure that you will believe my story. There were times when I had difficulty believing it myself. But I lived it. So I guess I really don't have the option of not believing it. You, on the other hand, can decide for yourself. Regardless of your decision, I will be fine with it. After all, when you think about it, I can't control what you believe about my story. I can only tell it.

*   *   *   *   *

There was once a young boy who rang the bells at a small country church every Sunday morning. He was so very excited about doing his job, announcing to the community that the services were about to begin.

A man once asked why he did it with such enthusiasm when so few people actually came to the church. The boy replied, "It ain't my job to fret over whether they come or not! It's my job to ring the bell and let 'em know we're here!"

So this is me, just ringing the bell.

CHAPTER 1

Growing Up Covered in Dirt

I'll begin my story about a mile and a half down an old country dirt road in north Georgia.

It was a typical childhood. Or at least it was typical for any young boy who was raised by good, hardworking, undereducated people in the South. We did not have an abundance of anything other than family love. As a matter of fact, as I learned later in life, we were actually quite poor—at least by today's standards. But I never knew.

Since there was very little money for all of the latest toys and gadgets, my friends and I had to come up with creative ways to entertain ourselves. We didn't have video games with battle scenes. We went outside and played army. Our version of "gaming" involved looking for the perfect stick to play with—just a little longer than our arms. When we pulled off the leaves, and broke off the small branches at just the right spots, the "V" at the end of the stick would align perfectly above our shoulders and below our armpits like the stock of a rifle; the small twig in the center made a perfect trigger.

It was a time when youngsters could play outside all day on a Saturday, letting their cares blow away in the wind as they rode their bicycles. We could be gone all day without our parents feeling the need every half-hour to pick up their cell phones and text us on ours. That fact was especially convenient; neither cell phones nor texting had been invented yet.

We rode bicycles and built tree houses.

When summer arrived, the swimming hole at the Swamp Creek railroad trestle was one of our favorite gathering spots. We had confiscated a rope from my friend Jeff's garage and securely tied a spare tire to the largest limb of an oak tree that stretched over the water. Then we pulled that "tire swing" as far as we could, away from the water. Someone else would yell, "GO!" We took off running, like the start of a race, yelling as loudly as we could—holding onto that tire for dear life!

As we crossed the water's edge, we wrapped our legs around the tire and rode it until it reached its highest point over the water. Then at precisely the moment when the tire's forward momentum would stop, we let go and dropped into the creek. We did this every summer when we were young.

Some boys in attendance were extremely talented "show-offs." That made them very popular with the girls at the Swamp Creek swimming hole. The girls would giggle and point at the boys as they did their "Golden Egg Drop" into the creek. A "Golden Egg Drop" was a masterful feat accomplished by entering the water feet first, after completing a back flip from the tire swing. I have no doubt that a successful "Golden Egg Drop" from a tire swing into Swamp Creek would have made the highlight reel at the "Redneck" Olympics.

I was never one of those "show-off" boys—I often wished very much that I were. I was never the most popular. I was never the boy who was the focus of all the girls and their young crushes. And I was never the one who could do a successful back flip from a tire swing into a creek. I wasn't afraid, and always gave it a good effort. I could just never quite master the skills—neither tire swings nor girls.

When it came to girls, I would just get a huge lump in my throat, and smile as I blushed. And when it came to back flips into the water, I usually ended up hitting the water squarely on my stomach. Then I would stay under water long enough that my screams from the pain would just dissolve into bubbles and float to the surface.

I remember our first color television set being delivered, and the cartoons we watched on that Saturday morning. I remember watching first-run television shows that you and your family may routinely watch now on the syndicated networks: *The Andy Griffith Show, I Dream of Jeannie, Bewitched, Gilligan's Island, Get Smart,* and *Bonanza.* I couldn't decide if I had a bigger crush on Barbara Eden (Jeannie) or Elizabeth Montgomery (Samantha). However, when it came to the all-important question from *Gilligan's Island*: "Who do you like better, Ginger or Maryann?" I was definitely a Maryann man.

There were no cell phones, video games, navigation systems in your car, or social networks. The only Facebook we had was our school yearbook, which we called an "Annual." And instead of "commenting on your wall," people "autographed your annual" – usually writing incredibly gifted poetry like,

Roses are red,
Violets are blue,
Rotten cheese stinks,
Your feet do too!
Have a great summer!

—Signed, Your Friend, Eric.

And yes, many of my friends wrote the word, "Signed" and gave themselves the title of *"Your Friend"* before their name on all of their annual autographs.

I played sports. I was on the basketball team (which is really hilarious when you think of how tall I wasn't!) I ran track and threw the discus. I also played baseball, and was considered pretty talented. Pretty talented that is until our teams got old enough that the opposing pitchers could throw really biting curve balls. Curve balls ended my youthful dreams of playing major league baseball.

I was a better than average student but not the most outstanding. I was a better than average athlete but not the one college scouts sought out. And I showed definite signs of leadership. As a matter of fact, my teachers would often refer to me as a leader (I believe the term they actually used was "ring-leader").

My teachers really did like me, though. I was fun and full of mischief. They would usually laugh, shake their heads, and say, "I know you're *up* to something! I just don't know what it is!" Being "*up* to something" was the term used for that stage in any prank where the plans were made, and the actions were being implemented. However, the final outcome and the certainty of the guilty party was still a mystery.

They were correct. I was almost always *up* to something. They always wanted to catch me. But I managed to stay at least one step ahead of them.

I even had a coach tell me once, "Son, you are showing signs of great leadership. If we could ever get you leading people in the right direction… you could accomplish anything."

As I got older, I worked full-time jobs during my summers and part-time jobs during the school year. I graduated from high school, and entered college with the plan to become a teacher. Upon completing my master's degree, I got married to my sweetheart and worked while she finished her Ph.D. in biochemistry at a major university in Texas.

My timing was a little off for getting a teaching position because I was entering the market in the middle of the school year. But I still needed to work. So for my first full-time, post-graduation job, I applied for a sales position with an insurance company. At the time, I would tell people that I landed in a sales career by default. As I look back now, I prefer to call it divine providence.

I truly had no intention of being in sales—especially not in "*insurance*" sales. I thought all sales people were somewhat pushy, and that "*insurance*" sales people were probably the worst. One of my coworkers liked to say, "Thank goodness for those 'snake-handling' preachers in those backwoods churches in the mountains! Otherwise, we insurance sales people would be on the bottom rung of the social ladder!" I hated to admit it, but I somewhat agreed. (My apologies to all of you good, decent, and hardworking snake-handling preachers out there. I don't mean to be disrespectful. I know you have a tough load to bear.)

My sales performance at that insurance agency was stellar!

(In my best Don Adams/Maxwell Smart voice)
Well, would you believe my sales performance was good?
Well, would you believe adequate?
Okay, would you believe that sometimes my sales results were better than horrible?

(Note: earlier reference to the *Get Smart* television show. My wife says I watch way too much television. I am watching her now as she reads this. She is raising an eyebrow, smiling slightly and thinking, *mmm-huh*.)

Back to being me again. My performance was not stellar. It was far from it. I didn't mind the work, but I just didn't seem to excel at it. I liked the people I worked with, and I knew that I could make an excellent living there. But for some reason, I was not succeeding.

My lack of success on the job was increasing my stress level. The money I was earning was inconsistent. And I was afraid that my wife would start to see me as a failure.

She was almost finished with her degree, and we both wanted to start a family. But I really didn't believe we were financially ready for that. The financial problems, and the job problems, were quickly being joined by marriage problems.

I have read that life is lived forward, but only understood backward. I do believe this is correct. And, even though I am no theologian, I do believe that God has a master plan for us that is good. I believe most things tend to work out the way they are supposed to, as long as we are not so stubborn that we refuse to get out of His way.

As I look back on it now, I can see that everything happens for a reason. At least it did in my case.

But enough with the introductions. I need to move on and tell you about the amazing day that began to move my life, family, and success into a completely different direction.

It all began on a Monday morning, when my sales manager, Jack Amberson, had put a note on my desk saying, "Come see me in my office."

CHAPTER 2

Are You Looking For Me? I'm Not Him!

My stomach began to churn. That is the only way I know to describe the feeling that came over me when I read the yellow post-it note on my desk. "Come see me in my office." That was all that the note said. And it had Jack's initials at the bottom.

I consider myself an optimistic person. I generally see the silver lining and not the cloud. I don't think I've ever been unrealistic, but I have always looked for, and usually found, the good in life. However, that day was the exception.

On that day, I was sure that the reason Jack was calling me into his office was to fire me. I had been at the company long enough that I should have been making my sales targets. I was smart enough to learn the skills that I needed. And people liked me. But, for some reason, I was just not "cutting the mustard," as we used to say.

I asked Scotty, one of my coworkers, "Do you have any idea why Jack wants to see me?" Scotty didn't even look up. He just grunted the word, "No." In my mind, Scotty's reaction confirmed my suspicions. *Scotty can't even look at me*, I thought. *Jack has to be bringing me in to fire me!*

I would love to tell you that I gave it some thought, and came to the conclusion that I was a grown man who could take responsibility for his own successes and failures. I'd also love to tell you that I walked uprightly into Jack's office, and humbly accepted his decision, shook his hand, and thanked him for trying so hard to teach me.

Did I "man up" and act like a big boy? Nope. I hid. I immediately went into the men's restroom, and stayed there for almost half an hour. Of course the situation only got worse. I thought about the humiliation of my failure. My mind raced and I forecast the disaster that would occur when I got home and had to tell my wife that I had been fired. I also played a movie in my head about when we would be getting those wonderful calls from bill collectors.

Finally, I worked up my courage, left the men's room, and walked into Jack's office. As I tapped lightly on the side of his door frame with the note in my hand, I asked, "Is this a good time?" I was desperately hoping he was too busy.

Jack looked up from his desk and said, with a smile, "Sure it is. Come on in and have a seat."

Jack was what we all referred to in the South as, a "good ol' country boy." He was always friendly. He was always there with a great big smile and a firm handshake. He genuinely seemed glad to see you every time you were around him.

His priorities were God, family, and country, and the evidence of this was all around you as you walked into his tastefully decorated office. His Bible was on the corner of his desk, and it had a worn and tattered look rather than a brand new "store-bought" look. Hanging on the wall, he had pictures of his wife, Sharon, and his young children, Ted and Becky. He had a couple of crayon drawings that his daughter, Becky, had made for him in frames on his bookshelf. On his credenza, he had a baseball trophy that his son, Ted, had won in the third grade. And, on a pedestal in the corner, he had a statue of an American Bald Eagle holding a flag.

Jack was also a "strapping" man. He had muscular arms that you could always see because he wore short-sleeved dress shirts and a nice tie. Jack never worked out at the gym. His muscular structure was because he was a hard worker at home as well as at the office. He did all of the "fixer-upper" chores at home. And he even helped his father with their family's farm.

Once, I accidentally helped Jack and his father at their farm. I say "accidentally" because I had no idea what I was getting myself into. Jack asked me if I would like to help them haul hay one Saturday morning. I had never done that before, so I said, "Sure!"

I showed up at seven a.m. on that Saturday, still sleepy. Jack and his dad had been up for hours. They were actually cheerful! I hadn't even had any coffee yet, and they were raring to go!

Jack got onto a flatbed trailer that was hitched behind a tractor, which his father drove. Jack said, "You walk behind the flatbed, and throw the bales of hay up here to me. Then I will stack them."

"All right!" I said.

And that may have been the last word I said for the next three hours. Not because I didn't want to talk, but because I was sweating like a racehorse on a hot day, and too out of breath to talk.

As I was struggling with my work behind the tractor, Jack was up on top of the flatbed— stacking the bales and making it all look really easy. He was joking around. And he handled those bales of hay like they were made of air! He was fifteen years older than me, but his stamina was putting me to shame.

Eventually, I tossed the last bale up to Jack. We then followed the tractor over to the barn. And I was truly relieved to see that the work was done. But, much to my surprise, Jack said, "Now comes the fun part!"

Jack continued. "I will get up into the hayloft. You stand on the flatbed and throw the bundles up to me."

Fun part?! I thought. *He has to be kidding!* I thought there had to be a machine to move the bales to the hayloft. I thought wrong!

For the next hour, I threw hay bales up to the loft. Jack caught them and then stacked them. There were a few bales that never quite made it to the loft. I began to believe that if the pain were any indication, I would wake up the next morning with my arms lying beside me in the bed—no longer attached to me.

And my hands would be making fists at me—crying, in sign language, of course.

The reward for the day's work came in the way of Jack's mother preparing a country feast for us. There were biscuits, fried chicken, potatoes, gravy, corn, okra, and other tasty treats. All of the items on that table had actually been grown or raised on their farm.

The family atmosphere was fantastic, too. Sharon and the kids were able to join us for lunch. And I watched Jack as his young children ran in and jumped into his lap. He gave them both a hug and a kiss and told them how much he loved them, and then he said something I will never forget. He looked at his children and said, "I am so proud that God picked me to be your daddy."

As we sat down at the table, Jack's family joined hands to say grace. I was sitting between Jack and his father. They reached in from either side and grabbed my hands to include me in their circle. Jack's dad said a short and simple prayer of thanks, and then we all dug in.

Laughter and great stories filled the lunchtime. Jack's dad loved to tell the stories of how nervous Jack was when he was getting ready to ask Sharon to go out on their first date in high school, and how he got even more nervous when he went to ask Sharon's father for her hand in marriage. We all had a good laugh at Jack's expense.

Jack's mother looked over at Jack and said, "Don't feel bad, son. Your father was so nervous when had that same talk with my father that he actually got physically sick."

Sharon smiled and said, "So did Jack!" Sharon looked at Jack and said, "Daddy saw how nervous you were. He liked you, but he intentionally stayed stone-faced through the entire thing."

Then with a big smile she said, teasingly, "He told me that he gave you his blessing, but he also said he wasn't sure you would amount to much."

Jack laughed and said, "The jury may still be out on that one!"

Everyone nodded their heads in agreement, trying to look very serious... but then the whole group broke out into laughter.

Sharon got the sweetest smile, reached over and grabbed Jack's hand under the table, and looked around the room—stopping first at their children, and then turning her attention back to her husband. She then gave Jack a little wink and said, "Oh, I think you turned our all right." I had to admit, I agreed with her.

Jack and Sharon had a great family. That tradition was obviously how they had both been raised, and they were passing it along very well to their children.

Like I said, Jack was a "good ol' boy." And he was a fantastic family man. That's why I couldn't understand why he would be sitting there smiling at me as he was getting ready to fire me!

Jack saw that I was anxious. He asked, "How are you feeling?"

"Stressed!" I answered, almost shouting.

He asked, "What seems to be the problem?"

Jack didn't know, but the night before my wife Jean and I had gotten into an awful argument. There was no doubt that she loved me and I loved her. But the tension between us was growing with each passing day. After paying for her tuition and repaying my student loans, there was barely enough money to pay the rent and cover basic living expenses. The lack of money just seemed to compound the anxiety I was feeling about my lack of success on the job; it was really hitting home in our marriage.

That anxiety was creating a very real physiological uneasiness in my stomach—a feeling I was not used to and didn't like at all. And, to make matters worse, I brought that feeling home with me.

Sometimes, the feeling we associate with stress and anxiety can still be with us, even after the event that created the stress is over. Then we often respond to other people—"innocent bystanders"—

as if the event is still happening, and they were the ones who caused it. That was exactly what had happened that night.

Jean and I were at the dinner table. I was thinking about the calls I needed to make on the next day, and I was enjoying an unhealthy dose of stomach fun just thinking about it.

Jean said, "This weekend, I need to go to the store and buy some new shoes." Note that she didn't say, "I am going to go out and beat your car with a sledgehammer." Nor did she say, "I think your mother is a total nag!" She simply said, "This weekend, I need to go to the store and buy some new shoes."

But because the way I was feeling inside, I responded to her as if she were the total cause of all my problems and her need for shoes was equivalent to family treason. I made the one person who loved me the most, and who was a totally innocent party, feel the brunt of my frustrations.

I can't remember exactly what I said. (Actually, I am just too embarrassed to repeat it.) But Jean left the table in tears, saying that she was starting to wonder if our getting married had been a big mistake.

So when Jack asked, "What seems to be the problem?" I just unloaded like a windstorm. I told him that I was stressed because I knew I wasn't making things happen. I was stressed because I thought I was letting him down. I was stressed because I was letting my wife down. I was stressed because I wasn't making enough money.

Basically, I was talking too fast, and saying too much. But I needed to let it out.

Jack's smile disappeared, but his expression still surprised me. It was not one of disappointment or anger. He had a gentler look about him. It was the look of a father or brother, or close friend who wanted to help.

Jack said, "Jim, do you like working here?"

I said, "Yes." And I really did.

He said, "Do you think you can learn the job?"

Again, I replied, "Yes."

He told me, "Well, you are not afraid of hard work. I have seen that firsthand." Then he leaned forward in his chair and asked me, "Why isn't this working for you?"

That is an interesting question, I thought. After all, Jack was my sales manager. Shouldn't he be *telling* me why it wasn't working for me, instead of *asking* me?

I looked down and said, "I really don't have an answer for you on that, Jack."

Jack didn't say anything for a couple of minutes, as he thought. Then he looked at me with a small grin and said, "I have an assignment for you."

"Okay," I said. "What do you want me to do?"

To my surprise, he said, "Take the rest of the day off!"

"Are you serious?" was all I could say.

"Absolutely," Jack said. "But there is a catch." Then he pulled out a twenty-dollar bill from his wallet and pushed it across his desk toward me. "I want you to take this twenty, and go through a drive-thru somewhere and get you some lunch. Then I want you to take the lunch to Cypress Park and eat it as you sit outside in the sunshine. While you are there, I want you to think about your situation and find a solution."

Then he bent over a little closer, dropped his voice, and said, "And I also want you to find a total stranger and do something nice for them today."

I was silent. I thought about asking, "What?!" But I changed my mind. The instructions were simple enough, and it was obvious that Jack really thought I needed to do some soul-searching.

So I slowly reached for the twenty on the desk, and pulled it toward me.

"Yes, sir," I said, quietly. And I got up from my chair and began to leave Jack's office. At the door, I turned around holding up the twenty and said, "Thanks for lunch."

"You're welcome," Jack said, as the smile returned to his face. But this time the smile seemed to have a little mischief in it.

I turned around and walked out of the office. I didn't say a word to anyone as I left. I don't even remember if anyone noticed me. I just walked outside, got into my car, and began to drive toward what would be the beginning of one of the most amazing adventures of my life.

CHAPTER 3

I See Invisible People!

It is just an afternoon off, right? At least that is what I was hoping as I drove out of our parking lot, turning right and heading down the feeder-road onto I-45 South.

I was still replaying the meeting in Jack's office. I thought his assignment was a little odd, but at least he didn't actually fire me. But that little smile on his face as I left had me puzzled. It reminded me of when my teachers thought I was *up* to something.

I just dismissed the thought, and continued toward lunch. It was a nice day, with blue skies and a temperature around seventy-five degrees. The humidity was low, and that was an unusual and nice bonus for Houston. I rolled my window down to enjoy the breeze. However, I didn't turn on the radio or play a CD. I just drove in silence, except for the sound of the cool breeze and all of the conversations that were taking place inside my head.

As I approached the Greens Road exit, I moved into the left lane in order to make a U-Turn and go back up I-45 North.

The underpass at Greens Road and I-45 is almost always a gathering place for a few homeless people when the weather is nice. Usually you will see anywhere from two to six of them holding their signs, and dressed in what would have certainly been really cheap clothing— even several years prior. Now the clothing was nothing much more than time-worn rags.

Actually, I said that you could usually see homeless people there. But the sad truth is that I had driven by that underpass many times during that year, and I almost never really saw anyone. As they were standing there, I would barely give them a glance. More often than not, I would actually avoid eye contact with them completely. Once I heard the morning news using the term *invisible people* to describe the homeless. I suppose that term accurately describes how I viewed them. I was uncomfortable. I was a little concerned for my safety. And I tried not to see them.

As I look back, I am reminded of the times when I was a child, and I was convinced that I could hide from my mother by closing my eyes. She would call for me, but I wouldn't move a muscle. I would just stand there, clinching my eyes shut—often while standing in the same room.

And when I would not come, she would ask, "Why are you just standing there? I can see you!" I would reply, "No, you can't see me! My eyes are closed!"

I think I was playing a similar game each day as I passed the homeless at the Greens Road underpass. I was mentally keeping my eyes closed, so that they couldn't see me. But this day was different.

I have a term that I like to use called "God Goose." Where I grew up, the word "goose" was interchangeable with the word "tickle." So if you tickled someone, you "goosed" them.

A "God Goose" is one of those moments when it almost feels like God is teasingly "poking" you in the side, like a tickle, just to let you know He is there.

Getting a very specific answer to a very specific prayer qualifies as a "God Goose." Or when the traffic light changes to green, but for some unknown reason you don't press the gas; then seconds later, a truck speeds through the crossing traffic and runs the light; that is most certainly a "God Goose." And sometimes a "God Goose" is a gentle nudge that is there to move you into a certain direction.

I am not sure if it was because of Jack's assignment or if it was a "God Goose," but on this day, my eyes were open, and I saw someone. The traffic light had turned red, and the traffic was heavy enough that I had to wait before I could make my U-Turn. So I was sitting still, with my window rolled down.

As I looked out my window to the left, there he was, just staring at me as if he knew me. He was an older black man that I estimated being in his sixties. As I would learn later, he was actually a decade younger, but the years on the street had really aged him.

His hair was a windblown mix of black and grey. He was wearing an old navy blazer that was tattered beyond repair. His shirt was plaid—the kind of plaid that could have been seen at a sock-hop from the 1950s. And his pants were khaki. At least I think they were khaki. But they could have just been covered in dust. His eyes were very dark.

We made eye contact and just stared at each other; neither of us said a word. No one moved. No one flinched. It reminded me of the old western movies where the gunfighters were "staring each other down" just before the draw.

After what seemed like an eternity to me, the light turned green, and traffic began to move. And as I traversed the U-Turn, we maintained eye contact for as long as possible. I could even see him in my rearview mirror, watching me drive away.

I was actually feeling quite relieved to be moving on. But then Jack's words came back to me. "I also want you to find a total stranger and do something nice for them today." I thought to myself, *There has to be another total stranger out there that I can do something nice for today. Maybe help an elderly lady across the street. Or maybe carry some groceries for someone at the local H.E.B. Grocery Store.* But the more I tried to argue my way out of it, the more I could see the man's face in my memory—and the more he could see mine, I imagined.

There was a local barbecue joint that I liked to frequent at the next exit. And even though Jack's instructions said specifically to go through a drive-thru somewhere, I decided to forego the typical drive-thru restaurants and get a brisket plate instead. I also decided to order an extra plate for the homeless man at the Greens Road underpass.

The lady behind the counter had on a nametag that said, "Eunice." (Of course it did! Every good barbecue joint has a lady around forty to fifty years old with sun-dried skin, whose name is Eunice. If you don't believe me, go down to your local barbecue joint. She is there, too. Ask for her by name.)

Eunice asked, "Will there be anything else, Darlin?"

I said, "No ma'am."

I gave her Jack's twenty-dollar bill to cover a sixteen-dollar check and said, "Keep the change" as I walked out the door.

I caught myself wondering if that extra money on the tip for Eunice would count as me doing something nice for a complete stranger. I suppose that I was hoping to let myself off the hook. But then I thought better of it. After all, Eunice wasn't a total stranger. I had seen her many times in the restaurant. And a four-dollar tip on a sixteen-dollar check probably wouldn't rise to the level of doing something nice for someone.

Not that taking a single meal to a homeless man would rise much higher. I mean, I certainly didn't expect the local news stations to come out and interview me after I took the homeless man a meal, and then broadcast my generosity on the evening news for all to see.

But I also knew that a four-dollar tip wouldn't mean as much to Eunice as that brisket might mean to a hungry man. So I did another U-Turn and headed back to the Greens Road underpass.

As I slowed down for the U-Turn, my eyes scanned the intersection. But my homeless opponent from my imaginary gunfight was no longer there. There were others, but none were making eye contact with me; I couldn't even give the lunch to one of them. It was as if I were the invisible man this time.

The car behind me tapped his horn to remind me that the light had changed. Disappointed, I drove away. I thought about coming back and making another pass through the intersection, but I didn't. I thought about giving the meal to another stranger. But I didn't do that either. I just drove ahead. In my mind's eye, I could still see that man and the way he looked directly into my face as I drove by.

I decided to go on to Cypress Park and have my lunch. Cypress Park is a beautiful small park in the northern suburbs of Houston. It has a full-sized soccer field, a baseball field set up for little league games, picnic tables, park benches, and well-maintained pavilions. And at this time of the year, the grass was a beautiful shade of green.

On the weekends, you will find families there watching the various sporting events taking place. You will hear people cheering for their favorite teams. You will enjoy the wonderful smell of hamburgers and hotdogs as they cook on one of the many grills. It is truly a slice of "Americana" and is one of my favorite places to visit.

On this particular Thursday, there were very few people at the park, and I was grateful. I wanted to have some quiet time to think about my conversation with Jack. I picked a park bench near a small stream that snaked lazily through the park. I sat down, and pulled one of my two meals out of the white plastic sack that Eunice had given me.

As I opened the cover on my Styrofoam lunch plate, a group of pigeons, which must have been almost directly behind me, suddenly and noisily flew directly over my bench. By instinct, I ducked slightly and then looked behind me to see where they had been. To my surprise, there stood the homeless man whom I had seen at the Greens Road underpass.

I like to think of myself as a "man's man," but I have to be honest and tell you that the hair on the back of my neck stood on end and a shiver went through me. Before I could utter a sound, he said with a loud Southern accent, "Boy! That ain't no drive-thru!" I didn't know what to say. I just sat there in silence with a stunned look on my face.

He said, in a calmer voice this time, "Boy. What's the matter? Cat gotch-yo tongue?" When he said "boy," he actually reminded me of my grandfather. It sounded like a cross between the words "boy" and "boa." It rhymed with the French word, *mois*.

I was beginning to relax a little. And I answered back, trying to sound much more macho than I felt, "You shouldn't sneak up on a man like that! This is Texas! You could get shot!"

He turned his head slightly and gave me a quizzical look that said, "Is that boy really carrying a gun?" Then a smile came over his face, and he walked slowly around to the side of the bench with a laugh that reminded me of many old men I knew in my youth. It was a slow and low laugh. "Heh, heh, heh, heh, heh!"

His voice got quite soft, as he looked down at the extra meal on my park bench and said, "Boy, you gonna eat both those lunches?" The look on his face told me that it may have been quite a while since his last meal.

I can't explain why, but my trepidation was gone. And I looked up at him and said something that I was sure would raise his curiosity. I said, "No. I actually bought this for you. But when I got back to the underpass, you were gone."

To my surprise, he had no questions or puzzled look on his face. He simply said with a smile, "Well, I'm here now! Let's eat!"

I got the other lunch out of the bag, as he settled himself on the other end of the bench. I handed it to him. He said, "Thank you," as he opened the cover and his hungry eyes saw the brisket. "This ain't drive-thru, but I'll take it."

I thought that comment was rather odd, but my thoughts were

more concentrated on how he could have possibly traveled from the Greens Road underpass to Cypress Park so quickly.

He looked up from his meal and saw me staring at him. "What?" he asked.

"I was just wondering how you got from Greens Road to here so fast?"

He just watched me for a few seconds, and then he looked down and said, "I really don't have an answer for you on that, Jack."

Now, I've never been a fan of street slang. I don't call people *Jack* just because I don't know their real name. But I have to admit that I was less concerned with what he said, and more concerned with how he said it. It was as if his thick, elderly, Southern accent was gone. And his cadence and voice inflection almost sounded like he was imitating someone.

That someone he was imitating was me. It was exactly what I said to Jack, earlier in his office. Before I said anything, he smiled and laughed again.

"Heh, heh, heh, heh, heh!" Then he shook his head back and forth several times as he went back to consuming his meal.

My mind was racing. I thought, *There has to be a simple explanation for this. Maybe he took the Metro bus over here. Maybe he hitched a ride with someone. But was he really imitating me? Or was I just imagining things?*

We finished our meals in silence—except for the occasional sounds he would make as he ate. One sound he made as he ate his meal was like a repeated low grunt. It reminded me of a frog in the pond back home.

He made another sound without opening his mouth. He would almost hum the affirmative words, "Mmm-huh." That was followed by, "That's good." And then another hummed, "Mmm-huh." As he closed the top of his Styrofoam lunch plate, he looked at me and asked, "Boy, why are you here?"

I thought about his question. Then I gave him a simple answer: "I'm having lunch with you."

"No!" he almost shouted at me as he shook his head back and forth several times. He was obviously becoming agitated with me.

"Boy! You don't follow instructions, and you waste too much time! Why… are… you… here?!" he said slowly, emphasizing each word.

I just sat there almost frozen for a few seconds. I just looked at this man—this homeless man I had only known for a very few minutes. I couldn't decide: was he was a delusional threat to me or was this just an eccentric old man? But since I really sensed no danger, I decided on the latter.

"Well, I guess I am here to figure some things out. My boss sent me out here to have lunch and to find out why things are just not working out for me right now."

I don't know why I was opening up to this stranger. But it did feel good to talk to someone who didn't know me. I would probably never see him again, so I didn't have to worry about being embarrassed later.

"I'm not getting the job done at work. I'm not getting the job done at home. I think I am in danger of getting fired. And my boss sent me out here to see if I can figure out *why*."

"That's right!" he said excitedly. Then the old man looked at me, and I watched his face soften. He said, "Boy, what's your name?"

"Jim. Jim Fariss," I replied.

"Well, Jim-Jim Farris. My name is Ray," he said as he extended his hand to shake mine. As I grabbed his hand, he said, "The first thing you gotta do is figure out *why* you are here." As he gripped my hand, it started to tingle. The sensation reminded me of the feeling that occurs when blood flows back into your hand or foot after you have been sitting or lying in a position that caused the appendage to become numb. As a kid, we referred to that numbness as your hand "going to sleep." And we referred to that tingling sensation as your hand "waking up."

As Ray touched my hand, it was if my hand began to "wake up." That feeling began to travel up my arm and, within seconds, the sensation had engulfed my entire body. I watched one of the pigeons as it was returning to the area. However, rather than the normal winged movement of a bird, it was moving in slow motion. And it was if I could see every flutter of its wings.

"What's happening, Ray?" I asked.

Ray laughed and said, "Don't worry Jim-Jim. You've been asleep. I'm just waking you up!"

At the time I had no idea how accurate the term "waking up" was going to be.

CHAPTER 4

You Gotta Find Your 'Why'

I kept my eyes on Ray's hand. As the tingling in my body began to subside, I could clearly see the wrinkled lines on his fingers and how his aged knuckles appeared to be swollen from arthritis. However, everything else in my peripheral vision was just a blur. I slowly began to look around and try to focus, but was really struggling to get my bearings.

"What is happening to me, Ray?" I asked

Ray replied, "You will get your wits about you soon. Just take a couple of deep breaths. The first time is pretty rough, but you will eventually get used to it."

"Get used to what?" I asked.

Something had changed about Ray. He looked the same. He had on the same old tattered clothes. His hair was the same. But his voice was different. Gone was the deep Southern accent of an old man. Gone were the ramblings that years on the street can bring. And gone was that look of a man who may not be totally in touch with reality.

Sitting on the bench with me now was a well-spoken man who was in full control of all of his faculties. He was actually much more in control of his faculties than I was of my own at that moment. As I started to speak again, Ray stopped me and said, "Just breathe, young man."

"Young man? Not boy?" I asked. He just looked at me with a sly grin. Suddenly, I heard the crack of a baseball bat, and we were no longer on the park bench. Instead, we were in the stands at the baseball field. And the park was no longer empty, but the stands were filled with people as everyone watched the game in progress. The smells and sounds of little league baseball filled my senses.

As I looked around in the crowd, I saw people smiling. Some were eating hotdogs. Others were eating popcorn. And all were cheering for their teams. Apparently, the game had been going on for a while, because the bases were loaded, and the scoreboard showed that there were two outs in the bottom of the ninth inning.

"How could I have missed the fact that this game was happening?" I asked. "I thought the park was pretty much empty except for you and me."

Ray gestured toward the game and said, "Watch the game. This is the fun part."

The speaker system crackled, and the announcer said, "Next at the plate, number 21, Jim Fariss!" I was astonished!

As I looked to Ray for some answers, the crowd began to chant, "Jim-my! Jim-my! Jim-my! Jim-my!" And a young boy, who I guess was about nine years old, walked up to the plate.

I said to Ray, "I don't know what is going on here! Is this some kind of mind trick or something? If we are supposed to be reliving some of my memories, you have it all wrong. I'm from Georgia, and I never played ball here. And I never wore number 21."

"That's not me!" I said, emphatically.

"I never said it was you," Ray said. He carried on the conversation without ever taking his eyes off of the game. "You are correct. This never happened to you, and these are not your memories."

I turned my attention back to the game, just in time to see young Jimmy take a swing and a miss.

"Strike one!" yelled the umpire.

The catcher threw the ball back to the pitcher, and patted his mitt twice. He then returned to his crouch and signaled for the next pitch.

The next pitch came in a little high to my liking. Apparently, little Jimmy agreed, because he didn't take a swing.

"Strike two!" yelled the umpire.

I could tell that young Jimmy wanted to look back at the umpire and argue, but he stepped out of the batter's box, tapped the bat on the ground a couple of times, took a deep breath, and returned to the plate.

There was no need for Jimmy to make his opinion known to the umpire. The crowd was making their opinions known well enough. The jeers were plentiful. The pitcher had the ball, hand in glove, and was looking down toward the catcher. He had an intense look of determination and competition in his eyes. His team was ahead by three runs, and all he needed to do was throw one more strike.

The pitcher took a short wind-up, and then hurled a fastball right down the center of the plate. Jimmy anticipated the fastball, stepped into the pitch, and released all the power his young nine-year-old body could give as he swung the bat.

"Crack!" The sound of the bat striking the ball sounded like a gun. The cheering crowd got suddenly quiet. But very quickly, the noise level began to increase again as the ball sailed into the outfield.

"Go! Go! Go!" they all began to cheer as the ball sailed further and further. And they erupted in excitement as the ball cleared the fence. Jimmy had just hit a grand-slam home run, and his team won the game!

I have to admit it. I had gotten caught up in the game by this point. I too was standing and cheering for Jimmy. I looked over at Ray and said, "You were right! This is the fun part!"

As I returned by attention to the field, Jimmy was rounding third base, and heading for home. All of his teammates were jumping up and down and waiting on him at home plate. As he touched the plate, the umpire shouted, "That's the ballgame!" as Jimmy's teammates did their best to lift him into the air. High-fives were slapping everywhere.

As soon as Jimmy was back on the ground, he immediately went running over to a man near the first base dugout, jumped up into his arms and gave him a big hug. The man was holding little Jimmy up off the ground and patting him on the back.

"Atta boy, Jimmy! Atta boy!" the man shouted as they hugged. "I'm so proud of you, son!" he said as a couple of tears slipped down his cheeks.

I couldn't believe what I saw next. The man turned slightly as they celebrated, and I got a clearer look at his face. I recognized him in an instant. He had a little gray in his hair, but there was no doubt as to who he was.

He was me.

I turned around to see Ray again. "Am I seeing things?" I asked "Are they who I think they are?"

"Well, that depends," said Ray, still watching the excitement with a big smile on his face. "If you think they are you and your son Jimmy, then yes."

"But I don't have any children!" was my reply.

"Not yet," said Ray.

Ray could see that I was obviously having a difficult time accepting all of what I was seeing.

"Where are we?"

"Wrong question, Jim. *When* are we would be more appropriate, don't you think?" He just smiled, and gave a quick wink. I said nothing.

Ray began to speak. "*Where* we are is *where* we were. Same park. Same baseball field," he said as he looked around the park.

"But, Jim, *when* we are is <u>not</u> *when* we were. This is your future, and that is your son, Jim Jr. And that man hugging his son is you."

Ray then looked down at my stomach and said, "By the way, you need to lay off the biscuits and gravy. You have put on a few pounds." He began to laugh.

I can't begin to tell you everything that was speeding through my mind. *Could this be real?* I thought. *Or is this just a hallucination? Is there some lesson for me here?* I didn't know quite what to make of it all. So I turned to Ray and asked, "Why am I here?"

"EXACTLY!" Ray said with a big smile on his face. And with that, he reached out his hand and touched my shoulder. Immediately, we were gone.

We were suddenly in an auditorium with the lights set low, and a spotlight on a stage at the front. Music began to play, and I recognized it as music from Tchaikovsky's *Nutcracker.* The curtain began to open and the ballet began.

I will admit that I have never been a fan of the ballet. However, for some strange reason, I was really drawn to this performance. And I was enjoying myself.

There was a particular young woman that I thought was doing an excellent job. She appeared to be in many of the dances, and had a grace and elegance that elevated her performance above her peers—at least in my limited opinion. Her physique was muscular but sleek. Her blonde hair was wound tightly and held up and into place by some beautiful small flowers. And her face was radiant.

At some point during the performance, I decided to relax about my adventure. I kept telling myself, *This is all just a dream anyway. I am still on that park bench, and have just fallen asleep. Just enjoy the show.*

As the ballet ended, the performers came out on the stage to take their bows. The young lady with whom I had been so taken was the last to hit center stage. The ovation of the crowd got louder, and the audience came to their feet as she bowed.

A man and a woman from the front row walked toward the stage with a large bouquet of flowers. The bundle was a wonderful and bright arrangement of red roses mixed with baby's breath. I couldn't see the couple too well from our vantage point, but I would have guessed that they were in their early fifties from their appearance. They presented the bouquet to the ballerina.

The dancer bent down to receive the flowers, and she kissed the man on the cheek ever so sweetly. Her smile was simply infectious. I couldn't help but smile right along with her. As the couple returned to their seats and I could see them better, I realized that again, I must be seeing my future. The man and woman were my wife, Jean, and me. I looked over at Ray and I asked knowingly, "What's her name?"

He smiled and said, "Whitney. Your daughter's name is Whitney."

"She's beautiful," I replied.

"Yes, she is," said Ray, with a pride that sounded like a father. It made me wonder if he had children.

"And so are your other two," he said as he pointed down front. "Do you see the blonde and the brunette sitting beside you? They are Lindsay and Haley. They're yours, too."

I looked down to the front, and saw Whitney's younger sisters applauding and cheering for her. I realized that I was really starting to enjoy my dream.

Ray said, "It's time to go." And suddenly, much to my disappointment, we were gone.

Instantly, we were standing at the side of Lake Conroe. It was early morning and the sun was peaking over the treetops on the eastern side of the lake. It was a cool morning, and there was a slight hint of steam rising from the unusually calm waters.

Ray bent over and picked up a smooth stone. Then he skipped it across the water. I think it jumped almost ten times. I looked over his shoulder and saw a small house made with beautiful Austin stone. The back patio faced the water and was covered in various flowers and plants. On the patio sat an elderly man and woman drinking their morning coffee. They weren't talking. They were just sitting there enjoying the view and sipping from their mugs. Gently, the man reached over and took the woman's hand, gave her a wink and a smile, and then returned silently to just enjoying the view of the water from their patio.

I didn't need to ask who they were. I simply asked, "Were we as happy as we look? Did we have a good life?"

"Oh yes," was Ray's reply. "Oh yes."

As Ray skipped another stone, he asked me, "Jim, why are you here?"

"At the lake," I asked?

"No Jim, on the bench." As he said those words, we had returned to the park bench. The park was deserted again, except for Ray and me.

I thought about his question and I said, "I am here trying to figure out why I am not succeeding at work... and, I suppose, why things aren't going that well at home either."

Ray asked, "Why do you do the things you do at work?"

I replied, "Because it is what Jack needs me to do. The company has targets, and it is my job to help make those targets a reality."

"That is where you are getting off track, Jim. You think you are working for Jack and his company. And because you are struggling, you are focused on it all the time. When you come home, your focus still doesn't change. Your mind is still on your job stresses, and that is hurting your family life.

"Listen to me carefully, Jim," Ray continued. "Your business is not your life. It is what you do for a living.

"There are some very rewarding careers that bring much value to life. But in *all* cases, the reason for a career is to give you the means to build your life.

"The reason you aren't succeeding is that you aren't doing enough of the right things, Jim. When that happens, the issue is a lack of motivation. And, if you have a lack of motivation, it is because you have not figured out *why* you are there. Because, Jim, if your *why* is big enough, you will be motivated enough to figure out the *how* in any career."

I think it was at about that point that the light bulb began to shine for me. As I thought about Jean, and the future Jim Jr., Whitney, Lindsay, and Haley, I finally understood.

"My family—my life: that is *why* I am in my job. They are my *why*, aren't they, Ray?" It was really more of a statement, rather than a question.

"That's right, Jim-Jim. That's right." As he answered, the Ray who had taken me on my magical journey began to slowly dissolve back into the Ray who shared my lunch.

"Boy, remember that the reason you do your job, and the reason you do ever'thang in your job, is not to build a company. It is to build your *why*. Jim-Jim, you'll always work harder to build yo' *why* than you ever will to build the boss-man's business."

And with that, Ray the tour guide gave way to Ray the homeless man. I sat there amazed at what I had witnessed. Ray got up, and began to walk away.

I stood and said to him, "Ray! Can I buy you lunch again? Maybe tomorrow?"

He looked back with a mischievous grin and said, "Sure 'nuff, but not tomorrow. Right here. Next Thursday." And he turned and walked away.

Without looking back, he waved his arm up in the air and yelled, "And bring drive-thru! Heh, heh, heh, heh, heh!"

I sat back down and looked at my watch. It was almost five-o'clock. I wondered if I was losing my mind. I wondered if Eunice had spiked my iced tea. I wondered if I would remember any of this tomorrow. But it was all so incredibly real to me. I laughed a little and thought, "Jean is never going to believe this!" And then I immediately decided not to tell her.

But just maybe, I would bring her to lunch here someday.

I wasn't sure of much. But I was definitely sure of one thing. I was going to be having lunch right there on that bench with Ray, next Thursday. And I was going to bring drive-thru,

"Heh, heh, heh, heh, heh."

*   *   *   *   *

On Friday morning, I went by the office as usual to begin my day. I felt rested after a good night's sleep. And I was actually look-ing forward to my workday. As I was putting some creamer into my freshly poured cup of coffee, Jack walked out of his office. He stuck out his hand to shake mine and said with a big grin on his face, "Good morning, Jim!"

"Good morning, Jack!" I said.

Jack then said, "Well you seem to have a little more spring in your step this morning! Taking the afternoon off yesterday must have done you some good." As we talked, he seemed to have a smile that reminded me of a mischievous little boy that had just put a fly in the teacher's lunchbox. But that is the way Jack smiled most of the time.

I sipped my coffee, and hummed my reply to Jack, "Mmm-huh." I almost chuckled when I realized that my reply was actually a pretty good imitation of my new friend Ray. Jack waited on me to comment about my afternoon. But I chose to remain silent. Fi-nally, he asked, "Well, did you figure anything out?"

"Maybe," I replied. "I think I may be getting a handle on it."

Jack slapped me on the shoulder and said, "I'm sure you will." And then he turned and walked back into his office.

I am not sure why I didn't tell Jack the details of my afternoon. I wasn't sure he would believe me. And I wasn't even completely sure that I believed it myself at that point. But I decided that keeping the experience to myself was the best course of action.

I went about my day and, I have to admit I didn't make any sales that day. Not even an appointment. I would love to tell you that everything changed immediately for me. But it just didn't happen that way. But, for some reason, I did have a little more spring in my step. And, although I can't say there was a tangible difference that I could describe in words, I truly felt better. I felt better about myself. And I felt better about my ability to succeed at my job.

My mind drifted back to something Ray had said to me on Thursday. He said, "Because Jim, if your *why* is big enough, you will be motivated enough to figure out the *how* in any career."

I took out a legal pad, and I wrote across the top of the page. "10 Reasons Why" And then I wrote the numbers 1 through 10 down the left-hand margin. I thought about all the reasons that I was working and why I wanted to become successful in my career. I began to list those reasons on the page. I only listed the personal reasons—not the business reasons. For example, I didn't list an income amount as one of my reasons for becoming successful. Instead, I listed what I would do with that income—what that income would mean to me and my family.

Although my top 10 "whys" have changed over time, I still take the time to read them daily. And I still have those original 10 reasons in my desk drawer today. They were not all that polished, but here they are.

10 Reasons Why

1. I want Jean to be proud of me.

2. I want to be able to give more at my church.

3. *I want to start a family.*

4. *I want to feel successful.*

5. *I want to raise my family in a great neighborhood with great schools.*

6. *I want to travel with Jean.*

7. *I want to be able to help my parents financially when they get older.*

8. *I want to always have more money coming in each month than I spend.*

9. *I want to be able to spend more time enjoying life than building my business.*

10. *I want to be a good role model for my future children.*

ACTION STEPS FOR THE READER:

The first step in becoming successful in any career is to spend time considering the question, "Why am I doing this?" Take time to list your top 10 reasons why you want to become successful at your career choice. Write them down, using only positive wording. For example, never write, "I want to stop running out of money." Instead, phrase it as, "I want to always earn more money that I need to spend."

Your list of 10 will change over time. But keep a current top 10 with you at all times, and read it daily.

CHAPTER 5

Work Ethic—Prepare to Win!

Jean and I had a great relaxing weekend, and I found myself ready for "the hunt" when Monday morning came around. Prospecting calls became easier. Appointments became easier. And when I received a "no," it didn't seem to sting as much as it had in the past.

I found myself really looking forward to Thursday and my lunch with Ray at Cypress Park. On Thursday morning, at around eleven-thirty, I stuck my head into Jack's office. "I'm headed to lunch," I said. "And I may be just a little late coming back in."

Jack glanced up from his spreadsheet and said, "Sounds good." Then he went back to work. And he muttered, "Mmm-huh. Sounds good."

Wow! I thought to myself. *Now everyone is starting to sound like Ray to me!*

This time I made sure to follow my instructions to the letter, and I went through the drive-thru lane at the local Chick Fil-A. I picked up two meals and drove to Cypress Park.

As I drove up, I saw Ray sitting on the park bench. He was talking. That seemed a little strange to me, since no one else was around. The closer I got, the more clearly I could hear him, deep into a discussion with himself.

"No, that's not what I said," Ray muttered, as he shook his head from side to side. "Yep! That's mo' better!" he said as he laughed. "Heh, heh, heh, heh, heh."

He must have heard me, because he stopped the conversation he was having with himself and yelled, "Hey! Jim-Jim! You got drive-thru today?"

"Yes, sir!" I said. "Chick Fil-A."

"That's good! That's good!" Ray said. "I like Chick Fil-A! Them cows think we should eat more chicken! Heh, heh, heh, heh, heh!"

We didn't say much as we ate our meal together. We just looked at the scenery and enjoyed the quietness of the moment. As Ray finished his meal, he crumpled his trash in the paper sack, tossed it into the trash can beside us, gave a loud burp, and said, "All right, Jim-Jim! Let's go!"

He put his hand on my shoulder and, in an instant, we were at my alma mater. We were in the back of a classroom filled with young students. As my head cleared from our journey, I recognized one of my college history professors, Dr. Thomas. He was at the lectern in front leading a great discussion on the free enterprise system.

As I looked around the room, I also saw myself sitting there. It was obvious to me that we had gone back to the first semester of my freshman year.

The Ray who had become my tour guide in this adventure replaced the Ray who had been having a "conversation" with himself on the park bench. His eyes were clear and comforting, and his voice had a deep resonance and assurance that told me this was not his first time inside a college classroom.

"Did you enjoy American history in college, Jim?" Ray asked.

"Yes. I did enjoy it. And Dr. Thomas was a great teacher!" I replied.

Ray asked, "Do you remember what grade you earned?"

"I got a C."

"You *earned* a C," Ray replied. His emphasis on the word

"earned" reminded me of an old commercial on television years ago.

"Okay," I said. "I *earned* a C. What's your point?"

"Who is that young lady sitting beside you?" Ray asked.

"That was my friend Gail. She was a great girl! She was really smart and always friendly. She even offered to help me study a couple of times, but I was busy with my fraternity brothers."

"Do you remember what grade Gail earned in American history?" Ray asked as he turned and looked toward me.

"I'm sure she made—I mean, she earned an A." I said as I smiled at Ray. "She earned an A in just about every class she took."

"Why did Gail earn an A, while you earned a C? You both sat in the same classroom, hearing the same information, from the same teacher, didn't you?"

I considered Ray's question for a minute. My first thought was to respond like a child and blame someone else.

The teacher liked her best! was what I thought. But I was old enough (and smart enough) not to say it aloud. I also thought about just saying, "Well, she was smarter than me." But I didn't think it was all that accurate. Finally, I just came clean with Ray.

"Ray, the truth is that Gail didn't earn an A by what happened in the classroom. It was by what she did outside of the classroom," I admitted.

"She studied very hard in every class. She told me once that the grades did not come naturally to her. She really had to put in the time after hours to learn the material.

"I really respected her," I said as I looked back at Gail.

Ray asked, "What is she doing now?"

"The last I heard, she had just gotten accepted into medical school. She plans to be a doctor."

"Mmm-huh," Ray replied. In the next instant, we were no longer in the classroom, but on a baseball practice field. We were watching the players take batting practice.

By this point, I was beginning to keep a clear mind as we jumped around, and I knew that we were watching my old high school team. I watched as my best friend, Brian, came up to bat.

"Hey! That's Brian!" I said to Ray. "He was always great at this game! We played together for years. He just got drafted into the major leagues!"

Ray looked over at me and snickered, "What happened to you?"

I smiled and said, "Well, as the pitchers got better, I just couldn't keep up. But Brian was a different story. Even when the pitchers could throw some great breaking balls, he could still hit that ball!

"He had a real talent." I said, very proud of my best friend.

"Talent?" Ray asked. And then he grunted, "Mmm-huh." And immediately the scene changed.

I looked around. We were still at the baseball field, but the sun was almost gone for the day. All of the players had gone except for two. Brian was still out there at home plate with a bat in his hand. On the mound was Gene, our best pitcher.

Brian said, "Throw me nothing but breaking balls, all right?" Ray and I stood there and watched as Brian hit ball after ball. I looked over at Ray and said, "Well. He did have a lot of talent. We both did. But I guess he also worked very hard to develop that talent."

"Jim," Ray began. "What do Gail and Brian have in common?"

I thought for a minute.

"They were both better than I was," I said with a slight chuckle. Ray was not smiling.

"Actually," I said, "I probably was as good as both of them. But they did things—extra things—that really helped them to develop their talent and excel."

Ray nodded his head. He asked me, "Are you familiar with the term, *Lagniappe?*"

I shook my head.

"*Lagniappe* is a term you will often hear in Louisiana. It is a Cajun term that means giving or paying a little more than is expected or required. Some people call it going the extra mile. Some call it going above and beyond.

"In the old days of the general stores, when someone was buying salt or flour, the clerk would put a sack on the scale. Then he would use a scoop to carefully fill the sack until it equaled the weight that was requested. Then, after giving the customer exactly what they were paying for, the clerk would pick up a smaller scoop, fill it, and then empty that scoop into their sack at no extra charge. That extra scoop was the *Lagniappe.*"

Ray continued, "I like to refer to *Lagniappe* as being that little extra that makes everything mo' better.

"It doesn't matter if it is work, family, or fun; always putting a little more effort in than others are willing to do separates the contenders from the pretenders.

"Brian and Gail were more successful than you, Jim, not because they had more talent. They were more successful than you because they were willing to work harder than you at developing that talent. They gave the *lagniappe.*

"Jim, there are a lot of talented failures in this world. And there are a lot of successful people that did not have as much talent, but were willing to work very hard to develop the talent they had."

Ray looked down at the ground and said, "And then there are people like you, Jim. People who have all the talent in the world but have yet to really do what it takes to develop that talent."

I looked down at the ground, shuffled my feet a bit, and felt embarrassed. I knew Ray was correct.

"But, Jim, if you take a person with that kind of talent, and you convince them to work hard—a little harder than everyone else—at developing that talent, then you have a superstar on your hands.

"Wasted effort is a bad thing, Jim. But wasted talent is a shameful thing."

Then Ray put his arm around my shoulder and said, "Boy, you can't expect a six-figure income if all you're gonna give is a minimum wage effort."

As I thought about what he said, I watched his eyes. He slowly changed back into my homeless mentor and we returned to the park bench.

I sat there for a couple of minutes, thinking about what he had said to me. Then I slowly got up. I looked at Ray and said, "Same time next week?"

He nodded.

I said, "I'll bring drive-thru."

"Mmm-huh," was his reply.

As I drove back to the office, I began to do a lot of soul-searching. I began to honestly evaluate my efforts at work and, I had to admit, I was doing the same thing that I had done my whole life. I was getting by on my natural talent, but getting by was all I was doing.

I began to consider what Ray had said to me, and how I could apply it to my life. My job wasn't hard. I knew the skills I needed. But I honestly had not put forth enough effort to become really good at those skills. I hadn't given the *Lagniappe*.

I also considered my home life. And I considered the type of home life I wanted in the future. I realized that I might be just getting by in that area as well. So I made a choice.

My choice was to list out all of the skills I needed to improve upon in order to be the best at work... and at home. I made a specific plan detailing how to improve my skills. I decided to find people I knew who were good at those skills and "pick their brains."

I started with Jack. I asked him if I could treat him to lunch on Friday. I asked him about his family life and about how he got started in his business. We talked for quite a long time. I don't really remember the specifics of what we talked about that day. But I do know that I began to learn with a different mind-set. And that mind-set has made a significant difference in my life. I now had the mind-set of giving the *lagniappe*—doing a little extra to build a life for my "whys."

Mmm-huh.

ACTION STEPS FOR THE READER:

What are the skills in which you must excel in order to become the best in your current career? Make a written list of the top 7.

Beside each skill, write out your plan of action that will improve you in each area. Write out the specific practices, the materials you will need, and the specific time you will devote to becoming better.

Identify someone you believe is excellent at the things you want to master, and take them to lunch. Ask him or her to tell you his or her story. Ask him or her why he or she is excellent at the particular skill.

Make a personal commitment to give the *Lagniappe* needed in order to become excellent at those skills you listed above.

Stay Connected with Jeff C. West

http://www.jeffcwest.com
http://www.facebook.com/jeff.west.330
http://www.linkedin.com/pub/jeff-west/87/2b4/473
http://twitter.com/JeffCWestAuthor

The truly great sales professionals and entrepreneurs are not born that way. They work very hard at their personal development. The Sales Tour Guide is a community of business owners, sales professionals and their families sharing information to improve the lives of everyone taking the journey.

Almost everything on the website is absolutely free for you to use.

Join us at

http://www.thesalestourguide.com
http://www.facebook.com/salestourguide

CHAPTER 6

Where Are You Going, Jim-Jim?

I have read many times that you tend to get what you expect to get, whether good or bad. And, while in my wildest imagination I never expected that anyone like Ray would become a part of my life, I found that the time we spent together, the surreal nature of the visits, and applying the lessons that I was learning was most certainly having a positive impact on both my work life and my home life.

I found myself expecting good things to happen—and they were. My sales results were increasing. That created a definite rise in my spirits as well as my bank account. That alone was also helping ease some of the frustrations at home. I was working harder, but the increase in my level of success was making that extra effort— the *Lagniappe*—well worth the effort.

On Thursday morning, I arrived at the office about an hour earlier than normal. No one else was there. Well, no one except Jack, of course. He was always getting there before the customary workday began for most folks.

"Well, you're here early, Jim!" Jack said, with a big smile on his face. He put out his hand, and shook mine enthusiastically. "Want some coffee?" I accepted.

As we visited around the coffee pot, I told Jack that I needed to come in a little early and respond to some emails before I went out on some sales calls. I also planned to get ahead of the traffic. I enjoyed the feeling of knowing that we were the only two people at work that early. I think Jack enjoyed that as well.

I drove into the parking lot of my first appointment at around seven-forty-five—about forty-five minutes early. Since I had the extra time, I decided that I would look around the area for other businesses. I made a list of each company, and made a mental note to ask my prospective client, Mr. Pierce, about them before I left the appointment.

As I was scanning the area, I noticed the Star of Hope Mission. The Star of Hope is a local shelter that houses and feeds the homeless in the Houston area. I watched as several homeless men and women walked about on the streets surrounding the building. I found myself wondering about their lives. I wondered about what brought them to the shelter in the first place.

I was sure that some were there as a result of some less than stellar choices they had made in their lives. But I suspected that others most likely had a story which, if known, would reveal much more than just the simple combination of their bad decisions. I also wondered if any of them knew Ray.

My thoughts were interrupted by the sound of my cell phone ringing. It was Jean.

"Hi there!" I said.

"Hi there back!" she said. "I just called to tell you that I love you."

I smiled, and said, "I love you, too."

"Okay. That's all," she said, and we said our goodbyes.

That was unusual, I thought. It was a nice surprise. Like I said, things were improving in all areas of my life.

As I ended the call, I looked back toward the mission and I saw Ray coming out of the Star of Hope. I started to go over and talk to him, but I thought better of it—partly because it was time for me to go in for my appointment and partly because I knew I would see him in a few hours. And because walking over into a crowd of homeless people was completely out of my comfort zone.

So I got out of my car and walked into the business for my eight-thirty appointment with Mr. Pierce. The appointment went well, and I was able to secure the sale. Then I left the area and made some cold calls closer to the Cypress Park area. It dawned on me later that I had totally forgotten to ask Mr. Pierce about the other companies in the area, and if he knew the owners. *Oh well, next time,* I thought to myself.

At eleven-thirty, I decided to make my way to the drive-thru of a local hamburger joint to get some lunch for Ray and me. "Two cheese-burgers—all the way—two orders of Tater Tots, and two large iced teas. Separate bags, please," I said through the intercom speaker.

"Swee— or —n-swee— on the —ea?" came the scratchy reply through speakers that sounded like they may have been stolen from a drive-in theater in the late 1950s. However, I had been to the restaurant enough that I knew the exact question the worker was asking.

"Unsweetened iced tea" I replied.

But then I decided to have a little fun with them. So I said in very broken syllables. "Wou— —u mind —stra —alt and —chup?"

The voice on the speaker came back as clearly and cleanly as an English teacher in high school. "Sure, extra salt and ketchup. No problem." I laughed a little, and wondered if the speaker was really working just fine but the waiter on the other end was entertaining himself by leaving out syllables when he first spoke to me.

As I pulled into the parking lot of Cypress Park, I noticed that Ray was not there yet. So I walked around and relaxed as I enjoyed the quietness of the morning. Finally, I saw Ray approaching the park. I held up the bags in both of my hands so that he could see that I had our lunch.

"Hey! Jim-Jim! What'd you bring us today?"

"Cheeseburgers and Tater Tots!" was my reply.

"No Chick Fil-A?" Ray yelled. "Well, score one for them chickens today!" He smiled a big smile.

"Mmm-huh," and shook his head as he laughed, "Heh, heh, heh, heh, heh." It was a laugh that now made me chuckle every time I heard it. We joined each other on the bench beside the baseball field.

As we ate, I told Ray, "I saw you this morning. I had a meeting near the Star of Hope. I saw you outside."

"Mmm-huh," he replied. "I stay there some nights. They're nice folks down there. Mmm-huh."

I sat quietly for a couple of minutes. I debated whether or not to probe further. I didn't want to invade Ray's privacy, but I really wanted to know more about him.

"Ray," I said, do you mind me asking? What's your story? How did you wind up at the Star of Hope?"

Immediately, I could tell that Ray didn't want to talk about this subject. He just stared ahead, and began to rock back and forth on the bench. Then he began to shake his head back and forth. I wished I had not asked. Suddenly Ray stood up.

"Where are you going?" I asked.

Ray continued to look straight ahead, and said, "That's right. Where are you going? And how you gonna get there?" He kept his gaze fixed at some unknown point before him.

I said, "Yes, Ray. Where are you going? And how are you going to get there?"

Ray turned slightly, cocked his head to one side, gave me a little sideways grin, and said, "Not me, Jim-Jim. You! Where are You going? And how are You going to get there, Jim-Jim?"

In an instant, we were no longer at Cypress Park. We were standing in Terminal C at George Bush Intercontinental Airport. For those of you who don't know, George Bush Intercontinental Airport is one of the nation's busiest airports. On average, over 100,000 people fly to, pass through, or leave from this airport on a daily basis. And Terminal C is one of the busiest sections.

It was obvious that we had "landed" in the peak of the rush time. People were moving in all directions. Conversations were happening on cell phones as people hurried through to make their connections. Small children were being fussy, and their parents' patience was wearing thin. Everyone seemed to be in their own little world. And absolutely no one noticed Ray or me. Before I could say anything, Ray nudged me forward toward the ticket counter.

"Where will you be going today, sir?" asked the nice young lady behind the counter.

"Uhhh," I replied.

I always sound extremely intelligent when I reply to a question with, "Uhhh."

My eighth grade teacher, Becky Epperson, always said, "Young man! Don't reply to a question with 'Uhhh'! That is the sound made by a brain that is in idle and not being used!" Becky Epperson was definitely correct today.

"Sir," the young woman said again politely, "where will you be going today?"

I looked over at Ray. And although the foggy-eyed look of my street friend had been replaced again by my always cognizant tour guide, he just looked at me and smiled. He was no help whatsoever!

"You are really enjoying this, aren't you?" I asked Ray.

"Mmm-huh," he said, as his smile grew bigger.

I looked back at the young woman. She also had a big smile on her face, and seemed to be amused at the situation.

"I have no idea where I am going, Miss."

She then gave me a wink and said, "Well, it is certainly going to be hard to get there then, isn't it?"

"Yes, ma'am," I said, somewhat embarrassed. "I suppose it is."

The young lady replied, "Well, how do you want to get there?"

"Uhhh," I replied again. Becky Epperson would not be happy. "What do you mean?"

"Well," she smiled. "Do you want to fly? After all, you are at an airport, sir. Or, would you rather take a train?" As she asked that question, our scene changed in a fast blur and we were standing at the ticket counter of Grand Central Station in New York. The noises of the crowd and the trains were all around. Before me was the same sweet young lady, but her uniform was now different. It matched the décor of the other train employees in the area.

I looked over at Ray. He had a different coat on. It was old and still a little tattered. But it was bright red! He looked at me and yelled, "All Aboard!"

"Well, I—" I began to speak.

"Or would a rental car be more to your liking?" she asked as our scene switched to the counter at Avis Rental Car. Her uniform had once again changed, and so had Ray's. They both looked perfectly at home, as if they had been working for Avis for years. Ray had started to chuckle as he saw my dazed look.

Not wanting to be whirled around again, I quickly said, "A rental car will be perfect!"

"And where will we begin going today?" she asked.

Tired of seeming totally ignorant and without answers, I replied, "Dallas! I'm going to Dallas!"

"Perfect!" she said. "Do you need a map, or maybe a GPS?"

Now, I have lived in Houston for a very long time. And on most days, I could make the drive from Houston to Dallas in my sleep—figuratively speaking, of course. But a few seconds ago, I was in Houston. And then I was rapidly in New York. And, at this point, I honestly didn't even know where I was.

"I'm thinking that a GPS might be a good idea," I said, glancing over at Ray. "I can use all the help I can get."

"Nice!" Ray said, as he opened the door to the car which instantly appeared beside us. Ray motioned me in, and I got behind the steering wheel. He walked around the car and got in on the passenger side. I looked over at him and said, "What's next?"

He just smiled and winked. "You're driving, Jim."

Okay, I thought. *I'll play along.* As I pressed the ignition button, the voice of the GPS began to speak. "Please state your destination."

At this point, I didn't trust my senses. But I would swear that the voice from the GPS was the same voice as the young lady who had been at all three ticket counters. After the beep, I replied, "Dallas, Texas."

"Please be more specific," the voice replied. "A general destination will not get you where you want to go."

"How about Reunion Tower in Dallas, Texas?" I replied.

"Is that a question?" the GPS voice replied.

I was slightly taken aback. "No. My destination is Reunion Tower in Dallas, Texas."

"Calculating route; Destination is set as Reunion Tower in Dallas, Texas."

"Great!" I said, but nothing happened. I looked over at Ray with a questioning look. He just smiled, and again was absolutely no help.

The voice came from the GPS again. "Well, start moving! Even God can't steer a parked car!"

"Wow! We have the world's first GPS with an attitude!" I said to Ray as I began to drive away from the parking lot. As I made my first turn onto the highway, my trusted little GPS told me every turn to take.

I jokingly told Ray, "This GPS reminds me of my wife. I never have to drive. I just hold the steering wheel. She does all the driving from her side of the car."

The voice of the GPS came back on. But it now sounded like Jean's voice. "I heard that!" it said. Ray and I both looked at the GPS with surprise. Neither of us said anything. But I heard Ray's now familiar, "Heh, heh, heh, heh, heh." After a few miles, we happened upon some road construction that made us detour from the route we were originally taking.

The GPS said, "Recalculating." It then gave new instructions based on the new information.

"That technology really impresses me," I said to Ray. "The fact that this little electronic device can link up with a satellite, plan my best route, and then make adjustments as needed based on unforeseen circumstances is amazing to me."

"That is very helpful when you need to get somewhere, isn't it Jim?"

"It sure is," I replied.

"Jim, where are you going?"

"Dallas," I answered. "Reunion Tower."

"No, Jim. At work, and at home: where are you going?" I thought about his question.

"Well, I want to make enough sales so that I can make the money to provide the life I dream about for my family."

The voice from the GPS said, "Please be more specific. A general destination will not get you where you want to go."

I was beginning to see where Ray was going with his point today. "You're right. I need to know the specifics of what Jean and I want to do for our family. Then I need to know how much income I need to make in order to make those dreams come true. And then I need to do the math, and define how many sales it takes in order to make that happen."

Ray asked, "If you know how many sales it takes to generate that income, do you also know how many presentations to decision makers it will take to generate the sales? And then do you know how many prospecting calls you need to make to generate those presentations?" I had to admit that I did not know those answers.

"Even if you know where you want to go, Jim, you still need to know how you are going to get there. So find out how many calls and presentations it takes to hit your sales goal. Track your activities and results. Then calculate your success ratios, so that you can adjust when needed."

The voice on the GPS said, "Recalculating."

The light bulb inside my brain was really starting to glow. I got it.

"I need to set my goals, both personal and business. I need to plan how many sales it will take to achieve those goals. Then I need to track those results week by week, so that I can make adjustments as needed to still hit my goals."

"Hmm-huh," was Ray's reply.

"Anything else?" I asked.

The voice came from the GPS again. "Well start moving. Even God can't steer a parked car."

"Hmm-huh," Ray and I replied simultaneously. And, again, we

were sitting on the bench at Cypress Park. As I watched my mentor fade into my homeless friend again, I said, "Thank you, Ray. I learned much from you today."

"That's good, Jim-Jim."

"That's good."

"See you next week?" Ray asked.

"I wouldn't miss it for the world."

ACTION STEPS FOR THE READER:

Set goals for your personal and professional life.

Determine the level of income needed to achieve your goals.

Determine the sales results required to produce the income you need.

Determine the activity level needed to generate the sales results required; be specific by activity type such as prospecting calls, presentations, follow-ups, etc.

Check with a trusted mentor; see if your activity levels match those expected in your industry to generate the needed sales results.

Break those activity goals down to what is needed on a daily basis.

Write your goals and activity plan down, and read them daily.

Track your results each week to see if your activity and results meet your industry standards. Use a map (track on paper) or use a GPS (electronic contact management system).

Adjust your activity plan if needed.

Then start moving. Even God can't steer a parked car.

CHAPTER 7

It's Not about You, Jim-Jim

Over the weekend, Jean and I sat down and made a list of the things we wanted to accomplish as a couple, and for our future family. We wrote them down on a piece of paper. And then we took some time to research the financial investment needed in order to accomplish those dreams. This list was very similar to the list of "whys" I had made previously. The difference was this time I included Jean in the process. That truly made it more meaningful for me. She really enjoyed the time as well.

I considered telling her about Ray. However, something inside kept telling me that it wasn't quite time.

On Monday I got to the office around ninety minutes early. I was hoping to beat Jack to the office. No such luck! He smiled as I walked in, and handed me a coffee cup. We visited for a while. I told him of my plans. I wanted to calculate the sales I would need to make in order to achieve my income goals. And then I wanted his input on the activity levels that would be needed in order to achieve the desired sales results. He was more than happy to help me.

Once my plan was written, and in my hands, I read it several times. I then headed back to downtown Houston. I needed to follow up with my sale on Thursday. I also wanted to ask the business owner, Mr. Pierce, if he knew the owners of any of his neighboring businesses.

My attitude was getting better and better. I was even enjoying Houston traffic that morning. It is amazing how having your goals clearly defined, and then having a step-by-step action plan that will help you accomplish those goals, will add excitement and enthusiasm to your outlook on life.

When I got to Mr. Pierce's business that morning, his receptionist told me that he got called out of town unexpectedly and would not return until Wednesday afternoon. I told her that it was no problem. And then I asked, "Could you give him a note for me?"

"Sure," she replied.

I took a thank-you card from my briefcase, and wrote the following note:

Mr. Pierce,

I have something for you. I will drop by on Thursday afternoon if that's all right. I would also like to get your input on something if you can spare 20 minutes. If there is a better time, please let me know. Thanks.

Jim.

I gave the receptionist the note and I left.

As I got into my car, I again noticed the Star of Hope. I had actually been doing a little research on them. I had heard good things about them before, and from what I had read online, I thought they were a very worthwhile organization. So I decided to get out of my car—out of my comfort zone. I walked over to the building.

I'm not sure what I expected to see. Maybe I expected to see a very depressing and gloomy world on the other side of that entrance. And, although you could certainly see despair in the eyes of some, you could also see the joy in the eyes of others. There were people who were receiving the services that Star of Hope provided. There were staff members who were coordinating various activities. And there were volunteers lending a hand. A woman came up to me and asked, "May I help you?"

"I was in the area and I wanted to come in and see what all you did here," was my reply.

She stuck out her hand and said, "I am Erma. I am the manager of volunteer services."

I shook her hand.

"I'm Jim. Jim Fariss."

"Well, hello, Jim-Jim Fariss!" Her words reminded me of Ray. "Let me show you around!"

We walked through the building, and she enthusiastically told me about the many services and ministries that came together at the Star of Hope. You could tell that she really had a passion for helping the homeless. You could also tell that she was very good at lining up volunteers. She was definitely a better salesperson than most. She tried to "close" me on volunteering twelve times during our ten-minute tour.

As I looked over toward the tables where several men were eating, I saw Ray. I thought he was making eye contact with me, and I offered up an awkward wave. He didn't acknowledge me in any way. It was as if he didn't recognize or know me at all.

"Do you know Ray?" Erma asked me.

"Kind of," I said. "We have shared a few meals together. But I don't really know too much about him. What's his story?"

"Well, we don't know very much about him either. And, even when we do know, we tend to protect their privacy rather than to share information."

I looked over to her and said, "He has become someone that I care about. Is there anything you can tell me?" I asked eagerly.

I am not sure why she did it. Maybe it was because she could sense that I meant no harm. Maybe it was because she wanted Ray to have someone checking on him regularly. Or maybe she just did it because she sensed it was the right thing to do.

"I am not sure about the truth in all of this. But I will tell you the little bit that we have heard over the years."

I nodded and listened.

"Ray apparently owned a very successful business in Houston for decades. We are not even sure what type of business it was. He was also apparently a very good family man.

"One day his wife and daughter came by his office for a visit. She had gone through the drive-thru at a local restaurant and picked up their lunch. And the three of them walked to the park at the end of the block to enjoy their lunch.

"When they finished their lunch, Ray walked over to the trash can to throw away their empty sacks.

"No one knows exactly what happened or why. But as Ray walked over to the trash can, two cars collided and careened out of control. One of the cars crashed into the bench where Ray's wife and child were still sitting."

My heart skipped a beat as I dropped my head. I fought back the tears.

"They didn't survive." Erma went on. "After the funeral, they say that Ray just walked into his business, put down his keys, took off his tie and he walked away. He never entered those doors again. He has been on the streets ever since," she finished.

I was totally caught off guard. I was completely breathless. I was also speechless—a very rare thing for me. I finally mustered up the courage to ask, "What was the name of the park?"

"I'm not sure, but I have always heard that it was Cypress Park."

I was stunned. I'm not sure what else we said that day. I suppose we both said goodbye and shook hands, but I really can't remember.

I walked back to my car. The tears that I successfully fought back inside the Star of Hope were now leaking from my eyes. I made a call from my cell phone.

"Hello," Jean said from the other end.

"Hi there, babe," I said slowly as I tried to regain my composure. "I just called to tell you that I love you."

"I love you, too. Is everything okay?"

"Everything is fine. I just wanted to hear your voice," I said. "I'll see you this evening."

I made my calls for the rest of the week. But I was totally distracted. Although I tried to keep my mind focused on what I was doing, I found myself continually drifting back to the Star of Hope and thinking about Ray's story.

It may have been because of my distractions, or it may have been just a mini sales slump, but that week seemed to be filled with more people saying "no" than normal. And I was a little too focused on what was not happening correctly, rather than what I should have been doing daily.

On Thursday morning I wanted to bring something different for lunch. But I was absolutely not going to do anything unless it came from a drive-thru. I happened to drive past the perfect solution. A Chinese restaurant was on the street corner near my last sales call before I headed to lunch. And it had a drive-thru! So I ordered two Mongolian Beef lunch specials, two soft drinks. As usual I asked for separate bags and headed back to Cypress Park.

My friend Ray was already at the park waiting on me.

"Good morning!" I said, trying to sound more cheerful than I felt.

"Hello, Jim-Jim! What'd you bring today?"

"Chinese!" I said as I held up the two bags.

Ray's face immediately showed signs of concern. "Is that drive-thru?" he questioned me.

"Yes, sir," I said as I smiled. "Wouldn't have it any other way."

Ray's face relaxed. "Heh, heh, heh, heh, heh."

We sat and enjoyed our lunch. We were mostly quiet today. It was a nice day with a few interesting clouds passing by.

"You seem kinda down today, Jim-Jim. What's the matter?"

I was determined not to let him know what I had heard about him. So instead, I opened up about the week I was having. "I've had a bit of a rough week this week. I have a lot of people telling me "no." I haven't hit my sales goals or my activity goals either. And I suppose that I am having a little bit of a 'pity party' over it."

"Them no's been bothering you, Jim-Jim? And have you been singing the blues?" Ray asked.

Then he began to sing, "*Nobody knows the trouble I've seen.*"

"Yes," was my simple reply.

Ray looked at me with an unusually serious expression. "It's not really about you, is it Jim-Jim?"

My mind began to race. I thought that Ray had found out that I had visited the Star of Hope and that I now knew more about his story. I didn't want to get into that and cause him to bring up some bad memories. But then, as usual, my friend surprised me again.

"Jim-Jim, I've got big news for you! Them no's don't matter! And it's not about you!"

In the next second, we were no longer at Cypress Park. We were now in Dahlonega, Georgia and, from the looks of things, I would guess we were somewhere around the late 1820s. I was surprised at how I was no longer shocked or disoriented as Ray and I took our journeys. I was actually enjoying the trips.

Not everyone knows this, but Georgia had its own gold rush that began around 1828 in Dahlonega. It is a beautiful little town in the mountains of the northeast part of the state. It is not too far from the beginning of the Appalachian Trail and Springer Mountain. The summer evenings are cool, and the scenery is outstanding. I was fortunate enough to get to hike in the area a few times as a teenager, and I have never forgotten it.

Ray and I were standing next to a small stream. In the stream was a man, stooped over with a pan in his hand—about the size and shape of a large pie pan. The man would put the pan down in the water, and scoop up some of the rocks and sand from the bottom of the stream. Then he would gently shake to pan from side to side and occasionally dip the pan down into the water.

"Do you know what he is doing, Jim?" Ray asked.

"I sure do." I replied. "He is panning for gold."

"How does that work?" Ray asked.

"He scoops up mud and rocks into his pan," I began. "And then he shifts it back and forth letting the lighter weight residue wash out of the pan. The gold tends to be a little heavier— and shiny, of course. So it will stay in the pan, and catch his eye. He will continue to do that until he finds his gold." As we watched, the man emptied the pan.

"No," he said as the water washed the last bit of debris away.

We continued to watch him as he repeated the process, pan after pan, always saying "no" as the debris washed away and the pan was empty.

"Jim, you mentioned that you have been getting more no's than normal this week."

"Yes."

"And you're bothered by that, Jim?"

"Yes."

"Why does a 'no' bother you so much?"

I thought for a minute and said, "Because I don't get paid anything on a 'no.' I only make money on a "yes."

"Yes!" The man in the stream yelled, as he held up a small nugget of gold. "That will buy supplies for the month!"

Ray walked over to the man and asked, "How many pans did it take you to find that piece of gold?"

"Thirty-one!" He was excited!

"That seems like a lot of work!" Ray asked, "Why didn't you give up during the first thirty pans?"

"Give up during the first thirty?!" The man seemed almost offended at the idea.

"The first thirty don't really even matter. What matters is that I was willing to go through thirty, or a hundred and thirty if need be, just to find the pan that had the gold in it."

"I don't get paid by any single pan. I get paid because I will go through ALL the pans to find the ONE that has the gold."

He continued to explain. "And, even though the one pan had enough gold to feed my family for a month, I don't put too much value on that single pan. Instead, I look at it like it took all thirty-one pans to find the gold. So really, it's like each pan that I went through, even if it had nothing, fed my family for one day.

"A day's food per pan is a pretty good wage, don't you think?" he asked, as he gave us a sparsely toothed smile.

Ray nodded and said, "Thank you!"

We turned around to walk away, and we were instantly walking into the ballpark at Atlanta Fulton County Stadium. It was a cool spring evening in April 1974. As we walked down the steps and took our seats, the announcer said, "Now at the plate, number 44, Hammering Hank Aaron!"

The crowd went wild! I got excited, too, because, growing up in Georgia, I knew exactly what I was about to witness. The Braves were playing the Dodgers. It was the bottom of the fourth inning. Al Downing was on the mound for the Dodgers.

"Cold Beer!" the concession worker yelled. I briefly thought about having one. I returned my eyes to the game just in time to hear the loud crack of the bat and to see Hank Aaron hit homerun number 715, breaking Babe Ruth's all-time record.

The crowd gave Hank a standing ovation that lasted for several minutes. It was one of the most exciting moments I have ever experienced. I felt like a kid again.

"He is the best!" I told Ray, "This was an awesome moment for baseball, and for Georgia."

"The best?" Ray asked. "Did you also know that Hank Aaron struck out over 1,380 times? Did you know that he also failed to get on base six out of ten times? And he failed to get a hit seven out of ten times."

I was almost disappointed in Ray. "Don't you get it?" I asked him. "It's not about how many times he didn't get a hit or get on base! It's about the times he did!"

Ray continued. "So, you're saying the times he didn't connect did not make him a failure. But the times he did connect made him a hero?"

"That's right!" I said.

"And it made him a whole lot of money, too!" Ray said as he showed me a big smile. I was beginning to see his point.

"Jim, you are conscientious and you really are trying to do your best. But you need to give yourself permission to not care about something."

"To not care about what?" I asked.

Ray continued, "You need to have the ability to not care if your prospect says yes or no. You are just like the gold prospector. You have to think of your prospecting as sifting through the no's in order to find your yesses. Then your yesses feed your family and provide for your dreams. You have to think like Hank Aaron: It doesn't matter how many times you strike out or fail to get on base. If you can get a hit three out of ten times, you are going to make a whole lot of money!" There was a spark in Ray's eyes at that point.

"There's something else, too," he continued. "You also need to remember a very important truth, Jim. It's not about you."

"What do you mean?"

Instantly, we were in an old hardware store on the town square in Denton, Texas. The wood on the floor creaked with every step. The smell of the old wood, along with the clanking of the hardware as people touched the various tools on the racks, reminded me of an era that is long gone but definitely missed. Progress has its casualties.

Ray and I watched as a young sales clerk and an older gentleman customer had a discussion. The young sales clerk began the conversation. "Sir, I have an excellent drill to sell you today."

"I'm not looking to buy a drill today, young man," the older man replied without any interest whatsoever.

"But, sir, this is one of the finest drills in the world. It comes with a lifetime warranty from the manufacturer. And it has three speeds."

"I'm not looking to buy a drill today," the man said, still not moving an inch.

"But, sir, you can't go wrong with this drill. It is truly the best made."

"I'm still not looking to buy a drill today, boy." The way he said "boy" sounded like Ray when we are back at the park.

The owner saw the exchange and came over.

"Hello, Tom."

"Hello, Bill."

"What brought you in here today, Tom? What is it that you need?"

"I need to put a hole in a board, Bill. That's what I need."

The owner looked down, and nodded his head.

"Tom," he said. "I've got exactly what you need to put that hole in that board. Take a look at this drill. It is the best made, and comes with three speeds and a lifetime warranty."

"I'll take it, Bill," said Tom.

The owner wrote up the order and took the money for the drill. The young store clerk was confused and a little frustrated. After waiting until the customer left the business, the young man said, "I don't get it."

"I know, son," said the owner.

And as he walked away, he shook his head and told the boy, "Tom wasn't looking to buy a drill. He was looking to put a hole in a board."

He continued, "You have to learn to find out what they want, then show them how what you have will give it to them."

Ray and I walked out of the store and onto one of the most beautiful town squares you will find in America. Shops and restaurants line the streets. And in the center of the square stands the majestic and historic Denton County Courthouse. The redbud and dogwood trees that surround the courthouse were in full bloom. In front of the courthouse was a small bench. We walked over and had a seat.

"Jim, when you make your sales presentation you spend too much time talking about you, your product, and what your product does. You need to stop that. God gave you two ears and one mouth. Use them in that same proportion. Ask your prospects questions to find out what they need. And then listen to what they have to say. If you ask enough questions, and if you listen well, you will usually find out that something you have will give them what they need.

"When you help them get what they need by taking advantage of something you have, you both win. They win by having their need met. You win by providing a service and getting compensation for doing so.

"Everybody wins when you remember it's not about you, Jim-Jim."

I thought about what he said, and I looked around the town square, only to watch it fade away into Cypress Park. Ray drifted back into my homeless friend.

"And one more thing, Jim-Jim," Ray began. I could tell he was struggling to stay coherent and give me another nugget of gold that day.

"The Good Lord blesses us so that we can bless others. The more good you do with what He gives you, the more He sees that and gives you more. Find something you believe in, and do good towards it."

"You can test Him on that."

"Hmm-huh."

As I drove away, I was very quiet in thought. Today's lesson seemed to be striking home with me on multiple levels. Maybe I had always been a little self-centered, but I hadn't noticed it before today. I began to think of all of my relationships, and searched for examples in which I looked out for the other person more than me. I was sad to admit it, but there weren't many instances I could find like that. It wasn't so much that I looked out for myself to anyone else's detriment. It was more like I just hadn't considered them at all.

As I drove up into the parking lot of my new customer, I began to think, *What can I do for Mr. Pierce today? What does he need?*

"It's not about you, Jim-Jim." I could hear Ray in my memory. An idea came to me. As Mr. Pierce and I entered his office and I sat down, I thanked him for his time and gave him some paperwork from our previous visit. Then I decided to ask him something as a direct result of my idea.

"Mr. Pierce," I began. "I want to thank you for your business. I really appreciate it. I make my living by gaining new customers and then taking good care of them, and that is exactly what I want to do with you."

"Thank you, Jim," he replied.

"Part of taking care of you, Mr. Pierce, is doing anything I can do that helps you do more business. I meet a lot of people as I prospect for new business and take care of my customers. I have a lot of contacts in the area. Would you mind taking just a few minutes to help me understand what questions I need to ask them, and what specifics I need to be looking for in order to know if they may be a potential customer that I could send your way?"

Mr. Pierce paused. He took off his glasses and laid them on his desk. And he just looked at me for a few seconds.

"Jim. Before I answer that question, I want to tell you something. In the thirty years that I have been in business, you are the first salesperson in my life who ever asked me how they could refer business to me." He went further. "All salespeople seem to want to gain referrals from me, but you actually want to give them to me."

"Thank you," he said to me.

We then had a lengthy discussion and he helped me to truly understand his business, who his potential customers were, and what I needed to know to send them his way. I actually had two customers of my own that I knew would immediately be good prospects for him. I called them while we sat there and told them to expect his call.

He then returned the favor, and asked how he could help me in the same way. I remembered my list of the companies that were near his business. We talked about each of them. He knew three of the owners. He pulled out some of his business cards and wrote a note on the back of three of them. They were addressed to the owners by their first names. And he wrote, "Jim is a friend of mine. Give him fifteen minutes." Then he signed each.

"Take these over to them. They will come out and see you."

I did exactly as he said. And all three of them came out to meet me. Mr. Pierce was able to turn both of my referrals into customers. I was also able to turn two of his referrals into customers of mine. The two of us kept referring business to each other for years, until his retirement. He even invited Jean and me to his retirement party.

As the days moved on, I found that the "no's" stopped bothering me. I actually began to get a little excited about them. I even went so far as to calculate how much money I made on every call based on my average sale. It was $48. So when I would get a "no," I would think, *Thank you for the $48!*

Once I actually said that out loud to a business owner who had just told me that he had absolutely no interest. I said, "Okay. Thanks for the $48," and I turned around to leave.

"What do you mean, thanks for the $48?" he asked.

I gave him a brief explanation of the thought process.

"I need to have you come in and talk to my salespeople!" he said.

"For a small fee!" I said with a big grin on my face.

We built a friendship and I helped him get what he needed. He actually did become a customer at a later time. It wasn't about Jim-Jim anymore.

The final words that Ray said were still on my mind. I needed to find something worthy that I could support, either with my time, my money, or both. I had a pretty good idea what it would be.

Hmm-huh.

ACTION STEPS FOR THE READER:

Determine the average number of prospects you must contact to make one sale.

Determine the average amount of income you make per sale.

Divide that income by the number of prospects you need to contact.

The result is the amount of money you make per contact. Remember that every "no" is still worth that amount of money to you.

Learn how your product fills a need for your prospect.

Determine what questions you need to ask the prospect to help him or her think through his or her needs and arrive at some conclusions about them.

Then make your recommendations based on what you have that fills that need.

Schedule "Give and Gain" meetings with your customers. Find out from them what you need to know about your contacts in order to refer business to them.

Refer business to your clients as often as you possibly can.

When asking for introductions and referrals from your clients, have them write a short note on the back of their own business card saying,

Ben. Jim is a friend of mine. Give him 15 minutes. John.

Use their business card as a note of introduction, rather than your own business card when you call on the referred lead.

CHAPTER 8

You Don't Know What You Don't Know, Jim-Jim, but You Can Learn

It was time for me to tell Jean about Ray. As I thought about that possibility, I will admit to you that I had a lot of trepidation. I knew that Jean was well aware that my job performance had turned around. I was making more money. We were talking about starting our family. And our time together was something that we truly enjoyed. Most of the stress and frustration had disappeared from our lives.

But I still had serious concerns that if I came clean about my adventures with Ray and how our lunches together had changed our circumstances, she might believe that I had completely lost my mind.

My weekly lunches with Ray had now been going on for months. I was learning new ideas and concepts. I was applying those lessons and making them work for me. It was as if I had my own personal coach. It was also a relationship that had grown into almost a family connection for me. Ray was my friend. He was my mysterious mentor. And I wanted Jean to know about him.

The weather was turning a bit cooler, as the month of October was in full swing. I have always loved the change of seasons. That always puts me into such a good mood. My favorite is that change from summer to fall. The heat finally dies off, football season arrives, and you know that Thanksgiving and Christmas are just around the corner.

On Thursday morning, as had become my tradition, I found a drive-thru restaurant and ordered our lunches. Then I headed to Cypress Park again. I got there ahead of Ray that morning. So I sat out on the bench reading through some emails, waiting on him to arrive. He never showed.

I waited. Ten minutes passed. Twenty minutes passed. But, still, there was no Ray. In the entire time he and I had been having lunch together, he had never failed to be there. For that matter, he had never even been late.

I decided that I would drive down to the Star of Hope and look for him there. As I made my way down I-45, my mind was racing even more than the traffic. *Is he okay? Did he forget?* I thought. My concern was mounting with each mile.

As soon as I could park, I hurried into the mission entrance. Luckily, I saw Erma immediately as I walked through the door. She saw me as well. She walked over to greet me.

"Have you seen Ray?" I asked. "We normally have lunch together on Thursdays, but he didn't show today."

"I wish I had gotten your phone number when you were here before," she began. "I would have called you."

My heart began to pound.

"Ray collapsed here on Tuesday."

"Collapsed? Is he all right?" I interrupted.

"Well, he is in the hospital," Replied Erma. "I don't know much more than that so far. We have been so busy around here, I have not had the time to go and check on him."

"What hospital is he in?" I asked.

"Ben Taub in the Medical Center area," she replied. "If you are going, please take my card. It has my cell phone number on it. Call me and let me know how he is doing." I took her card and left.

As I drove toward the Medical Center, I called Jean. "Hi, babe!" she said as she answered the phone.

"Jean, I just found out that a friend of mine is in the hospital. I am on my way there now to check on him." I said.

"Oh no, honey. Who is it?"

"It's a homeless man named Ray..." As I said that, for the first time I realized that I didn't even know Ray's last name. I had no idea if the hospital would be able to help me find him or not.

"A homeless man named Ray?"

"How do you know a homeless man named Ray?" she asked me.

"That's kind of a long story. I have been buying him lunch once each week for a while now. I will fill you in on the whole thing later. But I just found out that he is in the hospital, and I want to go and see about him. And I didn't want you to worry if I am a little late."

"All right honey," Jean said as we ended the call. "Keep me posted."

I barely remember parking in the lot at the hospital. I rushed through the front door and went immediately to the help desk in the lobby. I tried to calm myself down.

"I have a friend who was brought in here last Tuesday. I wanted to check on him."

"What's the name?" A perfectly logical question, I thought. I wished I had a perfectly logical answer.

"His name is Ray," I replied.

"Last name?" Another reasonable question.

"Well," I said. "That's the thing. I don't know his last name."

"And you're a friend of his?" She was now looking at me, with a raised eyebrow and a bit of skepticism. Who could blame her?

"Ray is a homeless man who was brought in from The Star of

Hope Mission on Tuesday. And yes, unfortunately I don't know his last name."

I felt somewhat ashamed of myself. I should have known.

"Do you know your name?"

"Well, of course I know my name," I replied.

"What would it be?" she asked me as she picked up the phone.

"Jim. Jim Fariss," I replied.

I suppose she could see the true concern on my face, because she asked, "Jim-Jim Fariss, would you take a seat over there while I make some calls?" She pointed to the chairs in the lobby.

"Yes, ma'am." I said.

I felt confident that either she was checking with the various nurses' stations to see if she could find Ray or I was about to be escorted from the building by the security officers. Fortunately, she was checking to see if she could find Ray.

After a few minutes, which seemed like an eternity, she motioned me back to her desk, and gave me directions to the intensive care unit section. As I was on my way to the nurses' station in the ICU, I noticed that hanging on the door of each hospital room was a small white dry-erase board. Each board had the name of the patient, along with various scribbling which I am certain meant something to someone who could understand medical code. Unfortunately, I was not one of those people.

As I was just about to arrive at the main desk, I noticed a room to my right. This board on the door of this particular room had the name "Ray—SOH" written on it. I assumed SOH indicated that he was picked up at the Star of Hope.

My eyes began to moisten as an orderly came out of the room holding some bed linen, and stopped at the board. She began to erase Ray's name. I couldn't believe what I was seeing. I had missed getting to the hospital in time to see him.

The orderly noticed me, and asked, "You know Ray?"

"Yes," I said. "He was a friend of mine."

"He's gone," she said, as she continued to erase the board.

"I gathered as much," I said, as I dropped my eyes toward the ground. "I wish I had known he was here." I was struggling to hold back my tears.

She looked at me with a confused look. Then, as if a light bulb went off inside her head, she said, "No! That's not what I mean. He's not *gone*. He's gone from this room! They moved him into a regular room this morning!"

"What?" I exclaimed.

She escorted me to the desk, and they gave me Ray's room number. I hurried through the hallways until I found his room. I didn't knock; I just walked into the room.

"Hey, Jim-Jim!" came the familiar shout of my friend. "Did you bring drive-thru today? This hospital food is terrible!"

Ray was sitting up in his hospital bed. He had various monitor cables that kept him tethered to the medical equipment beside him. But other than that, he looked quite well.

I gave a half-laugh and a half-cry. I said, "No, Ray. I didn't bring drive-thru. But I will certainly go get you some if they'll let you have it."

"They won't," he said. Then lowering his voice, he whispered. "We'll have to be sneaky! Heh, heh, heh, heh, heh."

To say that I was relieved would have been like saying Moby Dick was a nice little fish.

"When you didn't show up for lunch today, I got very worried about you. I went down to The Star of Hope to check on you. Ms. Erma sent me over here."

"Mmm-huh. I like Ms. Erma. I think she's sweet on me." As Ray mentioned Erma's name, he got a sly smile on his face and his eyes brightened up a bit.

"I don't doubt that a bit, Ray. Not a bit."

I asked, "Are you going to be all right? What are the doctors telling you?"

"I'm fine," he said as he gave me a look that seemed like he was a little embarrassed that such a fuss was being made over him. "They may take me back to the Star of Hope either today or tomorrow."

He said, "The doctors here are real smart. They don't have it right yet, though, that's why they're still *practicing* their medicine!" He had a big grin on his face.

"Ray, I think that is the only joke you have ever told me!"

"Mmm-huh," he said. "It's a good one too!"

"Yes, it was," I said. "Yes, it was."

"Do you think they will ever learn enough that they can stop practicing?" I asked.

"No," replied Ray. "Not if they're smart!"

He picked up the remote control, and pointed it toward the television. Naturally, my eyes followed along. As he changed the channel, not only did the program change, his hospital room changed as well.

We were in a library. It was not a new library, but a rather old library that reminded me very much of those I knew from childhood. The smell of old wood and old pages filled my mind with memories of Saturdays spent picking books from the shelves and reading the stories that were held inside. The shelves were tall, and there was almost no vacant space on any of them. Today, I often wonder if the technology of our digital world will someday make libraries a thing of the past. That makes me a little sad for our children.

I turned to look at Ray. He was still in his hospital bed. He smiled and said, "What do you see, Jim?"

As my eyes scanned the room, I began to list off the things I saw. "Books. Shelves. Files."

"No, Jim. Dig a little deeper."

So I walked over to one of the shelves and picked a book off of the shelf. The title was *The Magic of Thinking Big* by Dr. David J. Schwartz, Ph.D.

Ray said, "Open it. Tell me what you see now."

I opened the book to the table of contents. Then I began reading the chapter titles out loud.

- Believe You Can Succeed and You Will
- Cure Yourself of Excusitis, the Failure Disease
- Build Confidence and Destroy Fear

I turned to Ray and said, "I see a lot more than books on a shelf. I see where you learned many of the things you have been teaching me. I see some of the keys to success." Ray pointed the remote control again and clicked.

We were in the middle of a warm room. It resembled a den, or maybe a living room at a hunting lodge. There was a fireplace in the corner with a small fire crackling softly. As I looked around, I saw that we were not alone. Sitting in chairs around the room were some of the world's foremost authors on the subjects of sales, leadership, attitude, effectiveness, and self-image.

Bob Burg, author of *Endless Referrals* was there. Dr. John Maxwell, author of *The 21 Irrefutable Laws of Leadership* was there. As I continued to look around, I saw Stephen Covey, Zig Ziglar, Brian Tracy, Jack and Garry Kinder, and Josh McDowell.

I have to admit that I knew who these men were, but I was not all that familiar with their works. I did realize that I was in the presence of some of the best minds you could find on building your sales career, building a business, or just becoming a better person.

Bob Burg spoke first. "Hi, Jim! Is there anything you would like to ask us?" I felt like a kid in school who suddenly realized that he had forgotten to do his homework.

"I honestly don't even know where to begin," I said, somewhat embarrassed.

Ray said, "At this stage, you don't know what you don't know yet, Jim-Jim. But you can learn."

Zig Ziglar sensed my awkwardness and said, "Hey! Don't worry about it, kid! We all felt exactly the same way when he did this to us!"

"What?" I asked, as I turned back to see Ray. He gave me a wink and a smile. And as he did, we returned to his hospital room and once again, Ray and I were the only two people there.

"Wow! That's too bad! I would have loved to just sit around and listen to those men for a while!" I said to Ray.

"Jim. Do you read?"

Jokingly, I said, "Well, not that much… but I'm not against it!" Then I got more serious. "After working all day, I just never seem to have time to sit down and read much of anything."

Ray asked me, "Well, you just said you would love to sit around and listen to those men for a while. If I were to bring them back, would you make the time to do that?"

"I sure would!" I said, excited about the possibility.

Ray asked, "Why?"

I answered, "Because they have a wealth of knowledge that I would love to take advantage of. Their combined experience is overwhelming. I could learn so much from them."

"Would that be important to you, Jim? Say, important enough to make some time every day for it? Even after you have had a long work day?" I began to see where Ray was going.

"Jim, it obviously is not practical for these men to be your personal mentors on a daily basis. But they have taken the time to transfer their experience and knowledge into a format that you can have with you on a daily basis. It is called a 'book.' You may have heard of them," he said with a smile.

"If you would make time to visit with these experts in person, doesn't it make sense that you would make time to visit with these experts in their written words?"

"Yes, it does," I replied.

Ray continued. "Also, how much time do you spend in your car, stuck in our wonderful Houston traffic?"

"More than I like to think about," I said, recalling my daily drive time on I-45.

"And what do you listen to while in your car?"

"News, sports, and country music," I replied.

Ray laughed, "Well I don't blame you, Jim! The news is always good, your team always wins, and those old country songs are always so uplifting!"

Ray smirked and asked, "Do you know what you get when you play a country song backwards?"

"What?"

"You get your job back, your dog back, and your wife back!"

As Ray had a good belly laugh, I asked, "What's your point?"

Ray explained. "Those authors also have recordings that you can take with you and listen to in your car. You can have Bob Burg sitting at your side explaining how to generate a network of people that will refer business to you. You can have Zig Ziglar explaining how to close the sale when your price is not the lowest being offered. And you can have John Maxwell explain how to identify the real leader in any group you work with."

"Sounds like pretty good information to have," I said.

"That's right, Jim. And you can have it all. Invest in your future by developing your personal library of books and recordings from people who have expertise and skills that you want to learn. Then read and listen to them on a daily basis. And when you do have the opportunity to go and hear those people in person, do so."

Ray began to get sleepy. As he was nodding off, he made one final comment. "Jim-Jim, your trouble is not that you don't have time to read. You just have to adjust how you use your time. That's all."

And with that, my unexpected tour guide began to snore.

I walked away with a sense of relief because Ray was safe and well. And I also walked away with a new sense of clarity about how I would continue to learn and move toward becoming the man I wanted to be.

When I got home that evening, I sat down with Jean and told her everything. I told her how I met Ray. I told her how the success I had been having at work was directly related to the lessons I was learning from Ray.

When I finished, I told Jean, "I won't blame you if you think I have completely lost my mind." She didn't say a word. She just looked at me for a couple of minutes.

Finally she spoke. "Well, whatever has made the difference in you is a good thing. You are happier at work. We are happier at home. And we have a good future ahead of us." She leaned in and gave me a kiss.

"I don't know what to make of all of this, but I am going to get some sleep. And I am glad your friend is going to be okay," she said as she got up from the table and began to walk toward the bedroom.

She turned around and said, "By the way, Jack called. He said that you guys have your sales meeting in the morning. His wife normally brings something for breakfast. She can't be there to-morrow, so he asked if I would mind filling in. I told him I would."

"Good," I said. "It will be nice to have you there."

ACTION STEPS FOR THE READER:

Build your personal success library of books and record-ings.

Start with one book and one recording, and add to your collection each month.

Set aside fifteen to thirty minutes each day to read from your success library.

Use your "windshield time" in your car for listening to your success library.

Stop listening to the radio unless you have listened to at least one success library recording that day.

When you have opportunities to attend seminars to devel-op your skill sets in any area of life that you feel is important, invest the time and money to do so.

CHAPTER 9

Celebrate Your Successes

On Friday morning I got up early to have my coffee. As I walked into the kitchen, Jean was already in there preparing breakfast.

"Good morning," she said with a smile. "Want some coffee?"

"Yes, ma'am," I said as I gave her a quick kiss.

She looked up at my hair, ran her fingers through the unruly mess and said, "Your morning hair really makes a statement."

"What statement is that?" I asked.

She replied, "That hair says, 'This man could be the praise and worship music leader at any major metropolitan area church'!"

"Very funny," I replied. "You had better watch out, or I just may start singing!"

We laughed as she poured me a fresh cup of coffee. I sipped my coffee and quietly enjoyed my morning as Jean prepared breakfast tacos for our sales meeting. Jean has always been a great cook, and she loves doing it, especially cooking breakfast. Breakfast tacos are one of her specialties.

We decided to ride together to my office that morning. And as is my usual custom, I immediately reached forward and turned on the radio as I pulled out of the driveway. I remembered what Ray had said on Thursday. And, even though I had not yet acquired anything for my success library, I made the decision to leave the radio off.

As I pressed the off button, Jean asked, "Why are you turning off your news channel?" I reached over and put my hand over hers.

"No particular reason. Just thought I would rather hear you this morning. Your news is always better than theirs, anyway." Jean smiled at me in a surprised way. And then she just kept staring at me.

"What?" I said.

"Well, speaking of good news... I'm not sure yet... but I think..."

"What?" I said again.

She said softly, "I think we may be having a baby."

"Really? That is great news! Are you sure?"

"Well, I still have to go to the doctor, but I am pretty sure," she said.

"Wow!" I said, honking the horn. "We're having a baby!"

The car in front of me apparently thought I was honking my horn at them. They pointed up at the red light to let me know that they couldn't move forward yet. I held both hands up in an effort to apologize and said, "Sorry. But we're having a baby!" Unless the driver could read lips in his rearview mirror, he had absolutely no idea what the crazy man behind him was doing. But as the light turned green, he quickly scooted away.

Jean and I decided not to tell anyone at work until we got confirmation from the doctor. After all, it certainly made sense not to say much unless we were absolutely sure.

As we walked into the office, Jack gave Jean a hug and he gave me a handshake with a big smile and said, "Hi, Jean! Hi, Jim! How are y'all doing this morning?" With a great big smile, I immediately blurted out, "We're having a baby!"

Jean elbowed me in the ribs and said, "You just can't keep a secret, Jim Fariss!"

"Ouch!" I said, rubbing my rib cage. But then the smile came back even larger than before.

Jack said, "Fantastic!" Then he looked me straight in the eyes and said, "There is nothing better than being a dad. And you are going to be a great one!"

I was reminded of how Jack kissed his children and told them how glad he was that God picked him to be their daddy.

I smiled back at him and said, "I'm going to do my very best." Congratulations were circulating around the room. It was a wonderful feeling.

Jack got the sales meeting started as he always did. He began with a prayer of thanksgiving for the food, our families, the people he got to work with, and for his business.

Then he thanked Jean for preparing breakfast that morning. And he asked her to come up front for a special presentation. I thought he must have gotten her a little something as a gift for her preparing breakfast that morning.

Jack began to speak. "Jean, I really pulled a little trick on you this morning by asking you to prepare breakfast. I just used that as an excuse to get you here." Jean was puzzled. So was I.

"I'm going to give out a special award this morning, and I wanted you to be here for it. Jim, would you come up here for a minute, please?" I wasn't sure what Jack was up to, but I walked up to the front of the room.

Jack continued. "I have decided that we need to do a little better job in celebrating our successes on a regular basis. So, in addition to the great news you and Jean shared this morning, I wanted to bring you up and give you something. And, Jean, I wanted you to be here to share it with him."

Jack picked up a plaque and read the inscription:

Presented to Jim Fariss
For Outstanding Sales Performance
3rd Quarter Sales
Amberson Insurance Agency

Jack handed me the plaque and shook my hand.

"Jim, you were the top salesperson in the branch for the third quarter. And the turnaround you have made in your sales results this year have been outstanding. I want to thank you for your hard work."

Then he turned to Jean and said, "And, Jean, I want you to know how very proud I am of Jim. I know you are, too."

"I am," she said. She smiled at me and was a little teary-eyed. I was too. I've always been a bit of a sentimental old fool.

I don't remember much about the rest of the morning. We had a great time. We got a little business done. But we mostly just celebrated the successes we were having.

Jack had a meeting to get to, so he excused himself around eleven. Jean and I hung around for a few more minutes, and then decided to get out of the office and spend the rest of the day together.

I asked her, "Why don't we grab some lunch, and then head over to Cypress Park. I'll show you where I met Ray."

"All right," she said. "Are you going to get drive-thru?" She just smiled and laughed. I still wasn't sure if she believed me or not.

We talked about names for the baby as we drove. We talked about buying a home. We talked about our dreams. As I pulled into Cypress Park, I looked over to the bench near the baseball field. Much to my surprise, there was Ray!

"There he is!" I exclaimed to Jean. "That's Ray!"

"I'll take you over and introduce you to him!"

"All right," said Jean. "But do you think you should? He is not alone."

I looked again and could see that Ray was sitting on the bench talking with someone. The two of them were laughing and talking like they had known each other for a very long time.

"Is that Jack?" Jean said as she tried to see at that distance. As we got a little closer, I could see more clearly. "It certainly is!" I said. "It certainly is."

I imagine it would have been fine for Jean and I to go on over and introduce Jean to Ray. I don't think Jack would have minded. I think Ray would have loved it. However, I decided to just keep driving and not interrupt the moment between Jack and Ray.

As I look back now, I think I made the right decision. I learned some very valuable lessons from both Ray and Jack. But one of the most valuable lessons was found in what Jack did for me.

He passed the legacy of Ray on to me.

ACTION STEPS FOR THE READER:

Celebrate your successes

Give genuine self-praise for those steps in the right direction

If people report to you, celebrate their successes in public often

As you learn, don't forget to pass it along

EPILOGUE

In the office of Jim Fariss – current day

Derek tapped on the door to my office. He was a young man in his early twenties. He was likable, and full of promise. But this morning, he was obviously quite nervous.

"You wanted to see me. Is this a good time?"

"Sure!" I gestured toward the chair in front of me. I smiled at him and said, "How are you doing this morning?"

Derek looked down at the floor and said, "Well, not too good, actually."

He then began to open up and tell me about all of the stresses he was feeling. He didn't feel like he was living up to the expectations he had for himself or for me. He didn't know if he had what it takes to make it in sales. He finished by saying, "I've never failed at anything before. But I am starting to wonder if I can do this."

I asked him, "Derek, do you like this job?"

"Yes," he replied.

"Do you think you can learn the job?" I asked.

"Yes," he replied again.

Then I asked him, "Well, why do you think it is not working for you?"

Derek just looked down at the floor and said, "I'm not sure, Jim. I'm not sure."

I thought for a minute, and said, "I'll tell you what I want you to do. I want you to take the rest of the day off."

"What?" he asked.

"You heard me."

I took a twenty-dollar bill from my wallet and said, "I want you to take this twenty, go through a drive-thru somewhere and get you some lunch. Then I want you to drive out to Cypress Park, have your lunch, and spend some time seeing if you can figure out why you are not making things happen right now."

I slid the bill across my desk to Derek. Then I added, "Oh, and one more thing. I want you to find a total stranger and do something nice for them."

Derek picked up the twenty and slowly stood up. He had a questioning look on his face, but he never asked me anything. As he started out the door, he turned around, held up the bill, and said, "Thanks for the lunch."

"You're welcome," I replied as he turned and walked away.

"Mmm-huh. Heh, heh, heh, heh, heh."

About Jeff C. West

Jeff C. West is an entrepreneur with over 31 years' experience in sales, sales management, and business ownership. He has coached and led sales teams in multiple industries and has been among the top sales performers and sales managers in the nation.

For over twenty years, Jeff was in the voluntary insurance benefits industry with Aflac – the top brand and leader in that industry. As an independent contractor and sales coordinator with Aflac, he was able to find his preferred blend of business ownership and sales mentoring. He qualified for Aflac's Founders' Award For Management Excellence twenty-five times and qualified for numerous state and national conventions. Jeff recently retired from his position as an Aflac State Sales Coordinator after ten years in the Houston, Texas area, where Jeff led a team of over three-hundred independent agents and thirty-five sales managers to the "Aflac Top Ten" multiple times and qualified for Aflac's President's Club.

Although Jeff has lived in Texas for over twenty-four years now, he is originally from Dalton, Georgia, a small town in the northwest corner of the state. That blend of the two states that he calls home come together giving Jeff a story telling style that is both easy to read and highly effective at teaching principles for success in sales and entrepreneurialism.

Jeff has earned a B.S. Ed. from Jacksonville State University; a M.M. from Texas A&M University, Commerce; and a CLF® from the American College.

Jeff has two adult daughters, Lindsay and Whitney. They are

beautiful and intelligent; and will no doubt give him a big hug and a kiss when they read this. And he currently resides in the Houston, Texas area with his lovely wife, Laurie; she gives him a hug and a kiss every day.

www.JeffCWest.com
www.TheSalesTourGuide.com

Stay Connected with Jeff C. West

http://www.jeffcwest.com
http://www.facebook.com/jeff.west.330
http://www.linkedin.com/pub/jeff-west/87/2b4/473
http://twitter.com/JeffCWestAuthor

The truly great sales professionals and entrepreneurs are not born that way. They work very hard at their personal development. The Sales Tour Guide is a community of business owners, sales professionals and their families sharing information to improve the lives of everyone taking the journey.

Almost everything on the website is absolutely free for you to use.

Join us at

http://www.thesalestourguide.com
http://www.facebook.com/salestourguide